Success

Success

Theory and Practice

Michael Edmondson

BEP BUSINESS EXPERT PRESS

Success: Theory and Practice

Copyright © Business Expert Press, LLC, 2016

First published in 2016 by
Business Expert Press, LLC
222 East 46th Street, New York, NY 10017
www.businessexpertpress.com

ISBN-13: 978-1-63157-421-4 (paperback)
ISBN-13: 978-1-63157-422-1 (e-book)

Business Expert Press Human Resource Management and Organizational Behavior Collection

Collection ISSN: 1946-5637 (print)
Collection ISSN: 1946-5645 (electronic)

Cover and interior design by S4Carlisle Publishing Services
Private Ltd., Chennai, India

First edition: 2016

10 9 8 7 6 5 4 3 2 1

Printed in the United States of America.

Dedication

To Scott Edmondson, Lisa Pfeiffer Jones and Kathy Kitchener

Advanced Quotes for *Success: Theory and Practice*

"Michael Edmondson has written the handbook for those striving to succeed in the new millennium. Instead of a run-of-the-mill self-help book, *Success: Theory and Practice* connects the science, philosophy, and habits that drive individuals to success in today's marketplace. Success isn't a secret, and this book offers a roadmap for anyone willing to take on the challenge."

—Adam Cirucci
Political Consultant and Journalist

"Michael connects the dots in his book *Success: Theory and Practice* where the rubber meets the road with his 7 Characteristics of Success. He demonstrates the practical traits, backed up by fascinating research, to help you unfold your own success story."

—John P. Clark
CFP®–Financial Advisor and Retirement Living Expert

"Michael Edmonson's book is equal parts of research and vision. This is how we do success in the 21st century: not only do we seek to improve our lot, but also our relationships, our self-awareness, and our world. Success is not either/or, but both/and."

—Evan Harris
Co-owner of Tapas Yoga Shala

"Michael Edmonson's newest book is an absolute must read for both anyone entering the job market and those looking for growth in both their professional and personal lives. This book is not your everyday book on success, as it touches on the success of many, but lets you in on the mental and emotional challenges each faced throughout the journey. As quoted in the book from George Bernard Shaw "People are always blaming their circumstances for what they are. I do not believe in circumstances. The people who get on in this world are the people who get up and look for the circumstances that they want, and if they can't find them, make them." This book makes you want to find the circumstances you want in life."

—Rocco Marrari
National Accounts Manager for EBE Technologies

"Success: Theory and Practice is a must read for anyone who is interested in achieving personal and professional success. Personal and professional growth is a key to success in our careers in this ever changing environment. Dr. Edmondson provides questions to ask ourselves periodically as a performance temperature check along with some quizzes. He also provides real life examples of successful individuals and traits they implemented to achieve their success."

—Robert Sauselein, CHST
Northeast Operations Manager,
HazTek, Inc.

"Dr. Edmondson's writing style is clear and concise while including research relevant to theory and the practice of success. Choosing to read this book will challenge yourself to examine your own personal traits while receiving applicable advice on how to engage in successful behaviors, thus leading to personal and professional growth."

—Shelly Thomas Vroman
ICU Nurse

Abstract

The genre of self-help literature, often packaged as modern philosophy, sociology, and psychology, is a vibrant and growing $10-billion industry in the United States alone. For hundreds of years, authors have been helping people understand how to succeed in various aspects of life, including academics, health, finance, and love. Analogies, scientific research, autobiographies, psychological studies, and religious parables are just a few of the common forms of literature found along the spectrum of the self-help genre. During the last 20 years, however, the technological, digital, and information revolutions have connected billions of people around the globe and disrupted almost every aspect of how people communicate, live, and work. To help individuals learn how to succeed in the volatile, uncertain, complex, and ambiguous environment, today's technological revolution has helped individuals produce, access, and share thousands of research findings, publications, blogs, videos, online classes, e-books, websites, books, and other resources focused on some aspect of achieving success. When the three billion connected people around the globe are coupled with this hyper-production of information, an individual's cognitive capacity to process ideas is stressed and reduces the quality of decision-making. To improve an individual's capacity to process information, the self-help genre has a tremendous need for a publication that both summarizes the latest research and provides case studies. *Success: Theory and Practice* meets both needs and is valuable for any person interested in achieving personal or professional success. Divided into seven chapters, this publication provides a clear, concise, and compelling account on the theory and practice of success and includes research from history, psychology, sociology, cognitive neuroscience, animal behavior, and other areas. A list of readings, questions, and other resources are located at the end of each chapter.

Keywords

Success, theories of success, successful people, personal development, professional development

"We are not provided with wisdom, we must discover it for ourselves, after a journey through the wilderness which no one else can take for us, an effort which no one can spare us."

—Marcel Proust

Why Read This Book

In 1859, Scottish author and government reformer Samuel Smiles published *Self-Help*. A book that promoted thrift and claimed that poverty was caused largely by irresponsible habits, *Self-Help* sparked a new genre of literature over 155 years ago that continues to grow. With chapters on "Money—Its Use and Abuse" and "Application and Perseverance," it sold 20,000 copies in 1859. By the time of Smiles's death five decades later, it had sold 250,000 copies.[1] The genre of self-help literature, often packaged as modern philosophy and psychology, is a vibrant and growing $10-billion industry in the United States alone.[2] Since 1859, authors like Smiles and hundreds of others have been helping people understand how to succeed in various aspects of life, including academics, health, finance, and love. Any discussion of achieving personal or professional success today, however, needs to start with the driving force behind today's hypercompetitive global marketplace—the information technology revolution.

Dubbed "the most significant revolution of the 21st century" by Cambridge University political scientist David Runciman, the information technology revolution has altered, and will continue to alter, the very fabric of how people work, live, love, communicate, and do just about everything else in the twenty-first century.[3] *New York Times* editorialist and best-selling author Thomas Friedman echoed similar sentiment and declared the information technology revolution "the single most important trend in the world today."[4] Friedman summarized the impact of this revolution as the world went from "connected to hyper-connected during the 2000–2010 period thanks to cloud computing, robotics, 3G wireless connectivity, Skype, Facebook, Google, LinkedIn, Twitter, the iPad, and cheap Internet-enabled smartphones."[5] Technology is even moving into fields it previously could not handle, including intellectual and physical jobs such as performing discovery in lawsuits or preparing and serving hamburgers.[6]

During the 10 years from 2000 to 2010, world Internet usage increased over 444 percent.[7] The UN's International Telecommunication Union observed that one-third of the world's population, approximately two billion people, have Internet access. Just a short 10 years ago, only 300 million people had Internet access. Of the current two billion people with Internet access, 555 million have a fixed broadband subscription and 950 million have mobile broadband.[8] World population is expected to grow by over a third or 2.3 billion people between 2009 and 2050. If that occurs, by 2050 there will be a global population of approximately 9 billion people.[9] With more people alive, it is safe to assume the number of Internet users will continue to grow. For example, one estimate from the National Science Foundation predicts that the Internet will have nearly 5 billion users by 2020.[10]

The information technology revolution and the global transition from connected to hyper-connected has resulted in the creation of a volatile, uncertain, complex, and ambiguous (VUCA) global environment, creating an entirely new set of issues demanding that individuals develop their skills, commit to life-long learning, and improve their level of self-awareness. Eight in ten CEOs expect their environment to grow significantly more complex and fewer than half believe they know how to deal with it successfully.[11] Leaders from organizations large and small are more concerned than ever about the future because of the new requirements to lead in the uncertain and ambiguous 21st-century marketplace. Academic researchers have completed extensive research on how to help individuals and organizations achieve and sustain success in today's hypercompetitive, dynamic, and ever-changing global marketplace. Due to the vast amount of studies conducted, however, it is virtually impossible for anyone to become familiar with all of the publications related to success. Determining the exact number of success-related theories that academic researchers published during the last decade or two remains difficult to ascertain. One estimate suggests that there are approximately 28,000 journals across all academic disciplines publishing over 1.8 million articles each year; 90 percent of which are never cited by another author.[12] A small subset of those 1.8 million articles involves research on some aspect of success. Due to their technical design, limited circulation, and hyper-specific nature, half of the academic papers are read only by their authors and journal editors.

Success: Theory and Practice highlights some of the leading research on success and provides readers with case studies and questions for consideration. It does not, however, include all of the theories and recent research related to success. Doing so would be nearly impossible. Divided into seven chapters, this publication provides a clear, concise, and compelling account on the theory and practice of success and includes research from history, psychology, sociology, cognitive neuroscience, animal behavior, and other areas. A list of readings, questions, and other resources are located at the end of each chapter. Due to the substantial amount of research, many theories on success were excluded from this publication. Examples of research I chose not to include in this book include the role that physical beauty,[13] open innovation,[14] or how your partner's personality[15] factor into success. *Success: Theory and Practice* could easily be three times its current size. But that would be counterproductive to my objective of providing a clear, concise, and compelling account on the theory and practice of success.

Although there are many reasons to read this publication, here are the top ten. Read this book if you want to:

1. Understand some of the key success factors identified by researchers.
2. Define, or redefine, your definition of success.
3. Realize the connection between your level of self-awareness and your ability to succeed.
4. Recognize that many avenues exist in the pursuit of success.
5. Learn how others succeeded.
6. Ask yourself relevant questions challenging your dedication to achieving success.
7. Discover new theories on individual and organizational success.
8. Challenge yourself to think differently.
9. Examine the link between the theory and practice of success.
10. Grow both personally and professionally.

Contents

"Do something; do something to that; and then do something to that. Pretty soon you have something."

—Jasper Johns

How to Read This Book

Success: Theory and Practice is the byproduct of my research into successful people over the last 25 years. With a PhD in history, I realized the power of examining the backstory of a successful person. What allowed a politician to successfully navigate the landscape and get critical legislation passed? What enabled an athlete to perform a physical act previously thought impossible? What drove an artist to translate their vision into reality? These and many other questions fascinated me and drove me to research the backgrounds of many different types of successful people. During my historical research, a variety of research theories started to appear as I examined how people succeeded. Fascinating findings from fields unfamiliar to me like psychology, sociology, cognitive neuroscience, animal behavior, and other areas started to fall into view. Along the way I took notes and make connections. *Success: Theory and Practice* details that successful people demonstrate one or more of the following seven characteristics:

1. *Have a bias toward action*: Successful people have a bias toward action. They pursue what researchers have labeled deliberate practice, they demonstrate some level of maverickism, and they exhibit courageous behavior.
2. *Engage with others*: Successful people engage with others. They engage with a wide spectrum of people to collaborate, they leverage technology to connect with crowds around the globe, and they work and socialize in open networks.
3. *Commit to life-long learning*: Successful people are life-long learners. They possess what researchers have labeled a growth mindset, they understand the focusing illusion, and they develop their emotional intelligence.
4. *Increase your self-awareness*: Successful people increase their self-awareness. They practice a growth mindset, they understand the focusing illusion, and they develop their emotional intelligence.

5. *Remain open to the possibilities*: Successful people remain open to the possibilities. They work hard at determining their self, they understand how to market their value, and they practice meditation.

6. *Create options*: Successful people create options. They assess what is best versus what is right, they know how to turn a disadvantage into an advantage, and they engage in subtle maneuvers.

7. *Maintain a high level of energy*: Successful people maintain a high level of energy. They manage their fear, they practice deep survival tactics, and they perform under pressure.

The seven chapters of this publication examine specific theories and case studies related to each characteristic. After examining hundreds of theories, publications, and other resources, several conclusions started to become obvious:

- These seven characteristics consistently appeared in one historical investigation after another.
- Successful people often demonstrate more than one of these seven characteristics.
- Achieving success is the byproduct of both intention and circumstance.
- New academic and scientific research continues to improve our understanding of success.
- The ongoing technological revolution continues to disrupt previously established strategies to succeed while simultaneously opening up new opportunities for people to translate their dreams into reality.
- There is no one specific path to success.
- There is no secret to success.
- Success is open to anyone regardless of family history, educational background, or income level.

To understand these findings, review the backstory of the minions explained in the introduction. Doing so will illustrate the link between different characteristics and theories often found in the backstories of many successful people. A list of readings, questions, and other resources are located at the end of each chapter. If you are unable to answer all of the questions at the end of each chapter, I recommend that you at least examine your answers to the following seven questions, since they each relate to one of the key characteristics found in successful people. Select a time period (Ex: the last month) and challenge yourself to answer each question. Write down your answers and then revisit these questions and your previous answers each month.

1. Do you have a bias toward action?
2. How often do you expand your ability to collaborate with others?
3. What have you done to demonstrate a commitment to life-long learning?
4. How have you increased your level of self-awareness?
5. When were you open to new possibilities?
6. What have you done to create options?
7. What do you do to maintain a high level of energy?

Be honest with yourself when you answer these questions. Make a note to ask yourself these questions on a regular basis. Achieving a higher level of self-awareness is a critical first step to moving forward.

"If you want to succeed as bad as you want to breathe, then you'll be successful."

—Eric Thomas

Forward
The Definition of Success

Webster's online dictionary offers four definitions of success. The definition that most resonates with me and captures the spirit of *Success: Theory and Practice* reads as follows—"That which comes after; hence, consequence, issue, or result, of an endeavor or undertaking, whether good or bad; the outcome of effort." This definition of success is more than just a focus on the ends, but rather the means *and* the ends; the process by which an individual pursues a course of action that may or may not result in the desired outcome. *Success: Theory and Practice* helps us, as readers, realize the importance of self-awareness when engaging in the process; provides the tools and action steps to contribute thoughtfully and critically to that process; and offers insights into the role of our personal actions and engagement with others as key contributors to the outcome, whether the preferred outcome has been achieved (or not).

As an academic, I firmly believe in and live to be a lifelong learner though some days I am more successful than others. I subscribe to the Dewey definition of learning which focuses on the "struggle", and the result of that struggle is where true learning, personal and professional development, and growth intersect. But as I have evolved personally (now a mother of two) and professionally (nearing towards full professorship), my definition of success has also evolved. Context and time are great influencers of success and contribute to one's ability to be a life-long learner. Some days, success is showering and dressing my two and a half year old and one year old before noon (parents, I know you can relate). Other days, success is seeing a labor of love published or watching my students achieve their dreams and pursue their passions.

In a world in which work-life balance (an unrealistic expectation, in my opinion) and disengagement are even more challenging because of the ways in which technology makes us all too accessible, we need reminded of how to re-center ourselves by asking 'Why am I doing what I am doing?' as a quick, but all too necessary gut check as we recalibrate. Rather than rely on technology to perpetuate our "busyness" as a measure of success, we need to first be clear within ourselves what success is in the moment and realize success is always a moving target influenced by context and time. *Success: Theory and Practice* provides strategies, tools, and examples of how others' have achieved their definitions of success.

Perhaps even more important, Michael offers many definitions of success as measured by the individuals who embarked on their journeys rather than external influences. Much like beauty, success is all in the eye of the beholder. Unfortunately, technology allows others to "comment" on our successes in very unproductive ways, making the ideas shared in *Success* even more important and of great value. In our times of most need, we rely on models of how others have weathered and achieved their personal and professional successes. All the ideas shared in this book are doable, manageable, reasonable, and ongoing. Even better, they help us achieve Maya Angelou's simple, yet powerful words—"When you know better, you do better." *Success* not only gives us the empowerment to define and redefine success but it also helps us to know better, thus allowing us all to do better on behalf of ourselves and our greatest advocates and cheerleaders.

I hope you enjoy this book as much as I have, and appreciate the much needed reminder (much like me) as we all seek to be our best professional, personal, and spiritual selves as we seek to achieve *Success*.

—Vicki Baker, PhD
Associate Professor of Economics & Management
Albion College

"Success consists of going from failure to failure without loss of enthusiasm."
—Winston Churchill

Preface
The Changing Definition
of Success

In an article discussing the training of new radiologists, Dr. Richard B. Gunderman wrote that "everyone wants to succeed, but few people take the time to study success. Similarly, everyone dislikes failure, but few people invest the time and energy necessary to learn from their mistakes."[16] Dr. Gunderman's observation is an important one to highlight in the beginning of a book about success. The abundance of research on success makes it a field that people can indeed study. The *2013 American Express Life Twist Study* is one such example. In its research American Express discovered that nearly six in ten Americans reported that they consider themselves to be a success; yet 83 percent also agreed with the statement "I'm a work in progress." Most Americans today define their own success based on being healthy (85 percent), having a job they love (75 percent), having time to pursue passions (69 percent), continuing to learn and do new things (65 percent), and being able to make a difference in people's lives (62 percent).[17]

The study of success has a long history. The ancient form of Egyptian *hieroglyphs*, a formal writing system that combined logographic and alphabetic elements, told stories of specific episodes of success, survival, and other aspects of life. For thousands of years, as hieroglyphs evolved into alphabets such as Phoenician, Greek, Roman, Old English, and modern, people have been trying to define and explain success. What is it? How does one achieve it? What are the threats to achieve success? Does your definition of success change over time? How do different generations define success? These are just a few of the many questions on the understanding of success. Common definitions of success often involve the achievement of financial wealth, the accumulation of luxurious consumer goods, the acquisition of housing estates, and the collection of high-performance automobiles. The latest research suggests otherwise.

Current research indicates three emerging trends related to success. First, there here has been a "substantial decrease in the number of people who believe money is the only real meaningful measure of success."[18] A 2014 survey conducted by Ipsos interviewed 2,011 Americans aged 18 and older found that 67 percent associate success with achieving personal goals; 66 percent cited "good relationships with friends and family" and 60 percent said "loving what you do for a living."[19] Another new and emerging trend finds that the number of Americans who associate success with life experiences over the purchase of consumer goods continues to grow.[20] Moreover, during the last 30 years, Americans increasingly viewed life satisfaction, such as good health, finding time for loved ones, and creating a work–life balance as all signs of success.[21] Knowing that life satisfaction is now an important sign of success for many people, realize that "it's not about whether we have what it takes; it's about whether we choose to pursue it. The astonishing news is that for the first time in recorded history, it matters not so much where you are born or what your DNA says about you—today's hyper-connected global economy is waiting for you to step forward, with only the resistance to hold you back."[22] But will you? Will you step forward and translate your dream into reality? Will you take the necessary time to understand how to be successful? Will you learn from your mistakes? What are your dreams and more importantly, what have you done lately to translate them into reality?

In the global best-selling fictional novel *The Alchemist*, author Paulo Coehlo states "when people are young, they are not afraid to dream and to yearn for everything they would like to see happen in their lives. But as time passes, a mysterious force begins to convince them that it will be impossible to realize their Personal Legend."[23] A Personal Legend is one's destiny. It is the key to living a life of purpose and intention. Through the eyes of a literate boy shepherd, Santiago, *The Alchemist* proposes that the pursuit of one's Personal Legend exists as life's primary spiritual demand. As a result, the idea that all individuals should live in the singular pursuit of their individual dreams emerges as the primary theme of *The Alchemist*. Award winning author Laura Hillenbrand suffers from chronic fatigue syndrome yet pursues her personal legend of writing and achieved success for her books *Seabiscuit, An American Legend* and *Unbroken: A World War II Story of Survival, Resilience, and Redemption*.

As David Brooks of *The New York Times* wrote, "It is better to respect the future, to remain humbly open to your own unfolding."[24] If you can remain humbly open to your own unfolding, then you have given yourself an opportunity to experience what Victor Frankl called the space between stimulus and response. "In that space is our power to choose our response. In our response lies our growth and our freedom."[25] Remaining open to explore the space between stimulus and response might just ignite the personal or professional success previously thought impossible. Ironically, some leading researchers in the field of success have incredible backstories that demonstrate how they remained open to their own unfolding following tragic events. Amy Cuddy is one such example. Cuddy is an American social psychologist known for her research on stereotyping and discrimination, emotions, power, nonverbal behavior, and the effects of social stimuli on hormone levels. When Cuddy was a student at the University of Colorado at Boulder, she suffered severe head trauma as a result of a traffic accident and her IQ fell two standard deviations.[26] She had to struggle to regain the abilities she had lost, and when she returned to college as a 22-year old junior, she discovered a passion for social psychology.[27] Cuddy graduated from the University of Colorado at Boulder in 1998, began a job as a research assistant at the University of Massachusetts at Amherst and then earned her doctorate in social psychology from Princeton University in 2005.[28] Her TED talk entitled "Your body language shapes who you are," delivered at TEDGlobal 2012 in Edinburgh, Scotland has been viewed more than 30 million times and ranks second among the most-viewed TED talks.[29] As a follow up to her TEDGlobal talk, she published *Presence: Bringing Your Boldest Self to Your Biggest Challenges* in December 2015.[30] Cuddy remained open to the possibilities following a stimulus, her accident, and responded by dedicating her life to social psychology.

Questions and Resources

- How do you define success?
- When is the last time you thought about your definition of success?
- Has your definition of success changed over time? Why? Why not?

- How does one achieve success?
- What are the threats to achieve success?
- Does your definition of success change over time?
- How do different generations define success?
- Have you helped anyone achieve success?
- Why do people attempt to translate dreams into reality?
- What is the last book on success you have read?
- Have you thought about your personal legend?
- What has stopped you from achieving your personal legend?

Reading List: *The ABCs of Success Literature* list below highlights just a few of the many publications related to success.

Analogy: relies upon a story to convey lessons about success, self-awareness, and personal growth
- Paulo Coelho, *The Alchemist*
- Richard Bach, *Jonathan Livingston Seagull*
- Spencer Johnson, *Who Moved My Cheese? An Amazing Way to Deal with Change in Your Work and in Your Life*

Autobiographical: true stories of those who have overcome adversity to achieve a high degree of success
- Chris Gardner, *Start Where You Are: Life Lessons in Getting from Where You Are to Where You Want to Be*
- Farrah Gray, *Reallionaire: Nine Steps to Becoming Rich from the Inside Out*
- Blake Mycoskie, *Start Something That Matters*
- Sonia Sotomayor, *My Beloved World*

Behavior: research-based publications that focus on identifying the necessary traits and habits for success
- Charles Duhigg, *The Power of Habit: Why We Do What We Do in Life and Business*
- Daniel H. Pink, *Drive: The Surprising Truth About What Motivates Us*
- Susan Cain, *Quiet: The Power of Introverts in a World That Can't Stop Talking*

- Amy Cuddy, *Presence: Bringing Your Boldest Self to Your Biggest Challenges*

Cerebral: highlights the importance of what and how we think
- James Allen, *As A Man Thinketh*
- Norman Vincent Peale, *The Power of Positive Thinking*
- Mihaly Csikszentmihalyi, *Flow: The Psychology of Optimal Experience*
- Carol Dweck, *Mindset: The New Psychology of Success*

Collections: summarizes the backstories of famous people
- Joey Green, *The Road to Success is Paved with Failure: How Hundreds of Famous People Triumphed Over Inauspicious Beginnings*
- Tom Butler-Bowdon, *50 Success Classics: Winning Wisdom for Life*
- Darcy Andries, *The Secret of Success is Not a Secret: Stories of Famous People Who Persevered*

Examples: research-based profiles of high achievers
- Malcolm Gladwell, *Outliers: The Story of Success*
- Geoff Colvin, *Talent is Overrated: What Really Separates World-Class Performers from Everybody Else*
- Jim Collins, *From Good to Great: Why Some Companies Make the Leap. . . And Others Don't*

Exploration: emphasizes the importance of discovery
- Martha Beck, *Finding Your Own North Star: Claiming the Life You Were Meant to Live*
- Simon Sinek, *Start with Why: How Great Leaders Inspire Everyone to Take Action*
- Laurence Gonzales, *Deep Survival: Why Lives, Who Dies and Why*

Historical: uses lessons from historical events
- Caroline Alexander, *The Endurance: Shackleton's Legendary Antarctic Expedition*
- Jon Krakauer, *Into Thin Air: A Personal Account of the Mount Everest Disaster*

Intelligence: explains the role of intelligence
- Daniel Goldman, *Emotional Intelligence; Why It Can Matter More than IQ*
- David Livermore, *Leading with Cultural Intelligence: The New Secret to Success*

Inspirational: motivation is the key to success
- Anthony Robbins, *Awaken the Giant Within: How to Take Immediate Control of Your Mental, Emotional, Physical and Financial Destiny!*

Literature: classic literature texts examining personal growth
- Ralph Waldo Emerson, *Self-Reliance*
- Benjamin Franklin, *Autobiography*
- Sun Tzu, *The Art of War*

Money: solely focused on the accumulation of wealth
- Napoleon Hill, *Think and Grow Rich*
- Keith Cameron Smith, *The Top 10 Distinctions Between Millionaires and the Middle Class*
- T. Harv Eker, *Secrets of the Millionaire Mind: Mastering the Inner Game of Wealth*
- Robert T. Kiyosaki, *Rich Dad Poor Dad: What The Rich Teach Their Kids About Money That the Poor and Middle Class Do Not!*

New Age: spiritual in nature
- Eckhart Tolle, *The Power of Now: A Guide to Spiritual Enlightenment*
- Bevan Audstone, *Three Steps to Enlightenment*

Practical: lists and advice
- Stephen R. Covey, *The 7 Habits of Highly Effective People: Powerful Lessons in Personal Change*
- Richard Koch, *The 80/20 Principle; The Secret of Achieving More with Less*
- Jack Canfield and Janet Switzer, *The Success Principles(TM): How to Get from Where You Are to Where You Want to Be*

Relationships: focuses on connecting with others
- Dale Carnegie, *How to Win Friends and Influence People*

Secret: unravels the secret to success
- Rhonda Byrne, *The Secret*

Social Entrepreneurship: success is taking action and launching a venture that makes the world a better place
- David Bornstein, *How to Change the World: Social Entrepreneurs and the Power of New Ideas*
- John Elkington, *The Power of Unreasonable People: How Social Entrepreneurs Create Markets that Change the World*

Spiritual: how success is linked to a spiritual existence
- Viktor Frankl, *Man's Search for Meaning*
- Deepak Chopra, *The Seven Spiritual Laws of Success*

Task: managing to do lists in order to succeed in life and work
- Ken Blanchard, *The One Minute Manager*
- Brian Tracy, *Eat That Frog!: 21 Great Ways to Stop Procrastinating and Get More Done in Less Time*

Theoretical: theories that explain specific avenues to success
- John Kay, *Obliquity: Why Our Goals Are Best Achieved Indirectly*
- Tim Harford, *Adapt: Why Success Always Starts with Failure*

Women: focused on women and how they can succeed
- Clarissa Pinkola Estes, *Women Who Run with the Wolves*
- Sheryl Sandberg, *Lean In: Women, Work and the Will to Lead*
- Lois P. Frankel, *Nice Girls Don't Get the Corner Office: Unconscious Mistakes Women Make That Sabotage Their Careers*

Acknowledgments

Scott Edmondson, Lisa Pfeiffer Jones and Kathy Kitchener embody the traits of successful people. I dedicated this book to them because they needed to discover a way forward following tragic events. In less than two years Scott lost his father and two of his brothers and cared for his mother who was diagnosed with cancer. Lisa's husband died and she was left to raise their only child. Kathy suffered a devastating loss when her one year old daughter died of a rare illness. In a book about the theory and practice of successful people, these three individuals demonstrate by example how to succeed amidst the darkest of times. They succeeded because they choose to move forward. Their dedication to life, concern for others, and bias towards action have allowed them to succeed. They were each gracious enough to write a brief statement to be included here.

Kathy's story: "On the morning of 11 May I never thought I was saying goodbye to my beautiful daughter Kathryn for the last time. Kate died due to an undiagnosed tumor in her throat. It was a devastating loss. I never would have gotten out of bed the days following without the love and support of my husband. He made sure I was up, dressed, and ate. We supported each other since that horrible day. When I fall he is there to pick me up; and when he stumbles, I am there to support him. Many marriages crumble after the loss of a child. We have managed to keep moving, I always hated the phrase getting over a loss. We will never get over the loss of Kate. As we hold the love for Kate in our hearts forever. And because of our love for her and each other, we were blessed with our rainbow baby, Olivia, and will share our love and stories of her big sister. You never fully get over the loss or past the grief. I carry it each and every day of my life. I have suffered bad days and worse days since Kate's passing. Now I try to have as many good days for Olivia as possible."

Lisa's story: "As a West Point graduate, Keith embodied the ideology of 'Duty, Honor, and Country.' He also had a magical way of making people feel comfortable and respected. Never one to brag, the fact that he was a former cadet, an attorney and sang opera "for fun" remained a mystery to many. Our marriage was a true partnership. With his passing, I lost my husband, confidant and best friend. My life lost its laughter and its song. Moving forward, I prayed for patience, grace and strength. I knew I had to raise our son and understood there were no second chances. Looking in Andy's eyes, I recognized that every hope I had for his future rested on the decisions I made in the wake of losing Keith. In my heart and mind I purposely walled off the grief and focused on the stability and faith for the future that we both craved. I became a master at compartmentalizing and putting up a brave front when necessary, then crumbling into a sobbing mess when I was alone. Thankfully, over time, the stability and hope I worked so hard to create became my solace. In some ways, it was all an elaborate "fake it 'til you make it" scheme. As a side note – Both Andy and I found that helping others soothed our weary souls. We have participated in many volunteer projects, but feeding the hungry has become a passion. As Andy once said (while serving at the Trenton Soup Kitchen), 'We were just one life insurance policy away from being on the other side of the table.' His thoughts were a bit dramatic, but not completely unfounded."

Scott's story: "John Lennon said it best, 'Life is what happens to you while you're busy making other plans.' In a brief period of time I suffered a series of life altering events that made me into the person I am today. Starting in the fall of 2009 into the spring of 2010, I experienced the death of my father and two brothers, a diagnosis of endometrial cancer in my mother, and a divorce. During this time period, I honestly did not know what to think, other than I could not give up hope that things would get better. They say you go through five stages of grief such as denial, anger, bargaining, depression, and acceptance. However, my experience was that these stages were fluid and did not go in order. Additionally, I experienced embarrassment, doubt, anxiety, and confusion. However, this would not deter me. The one thing my father told me growing up, was not to give up. In my darkest days, I felt I owed it to him to bring his words to life. I worked my ass off during this time to distract myself and take my mind off things. I worked overtime, two jobs, and then life happened. When I least expected it, I met my beautiful wife Michele. She restored my faith in love, friendship, and family, and has blessed me with two beautiful children."

Thank you all for allowing me to use your stories in this book. Your commitment to moving forward serves as an example for others to follow. New Zealand explorer Edmund Hillary noted that "People do not decide to become extraordinary. They decide to accomplish extraordinary things." Moving forward amidst tragic death requires extraordinary effort. Kathy, Scott and Lisa are ordinary people who accomplished extraordinary things.

I would also like to thank Adam Cirucci, Evan Harris, John Clark, Rocco Marrari, Robert Sauselin, Shelly Thomas Vroman, and Vicki Baker Harris for their comments on a draft of this manuscript. To the entire team at Business Experts Press including Stewart Mattson, Rob Zwettler, Charlene Kronstedt, Lisa Blade, Sean Kaneski, Sheri Dean, and Karen Amundson I owe my deepest appreciation and gratitude for their constant support. *Success: Theory and Practice* is the third book that Business Experts Press for me as they previously published *Marketing Your Value: Nine Steps to Navigate Your Career* and *Major in Happiness: Debunking the College Major Fallacies*. I would also like to extend a special acknowledgement and thank you to my family and friends for their daily guidance and support including my wife Lori Joyce who made sure that our children Amanda Haley and Jonathan Victor continue to travel down the road to success as they mature.

Introduction
Linking the Theory and
Practice of Success

It is both useful and necessary to use a case study that illustrates how success seldom comes from any one specific theory. The individuals highlighted in each case study here rarely reviewed the research and then directly applied the findings to their life in order to achieve immediate success. Personal growth and professional development follow a far more circuitous route. When you examine the backstory of many successful people, organizations, and brands, multiple theories of success are often involved. Examining the backstory of the small, yellow creatures known as minions, who went from relative obscurity to a $1 billion brand during the last five years, seems like a good starting point. While the minions might have exploded in popularity and created one of the most recognizable and successful brands and images during the last few years, their path to creation started over five decades ago. What follows is a summary of how the minions came into existence with links to the various theories of success involved along the way: serendipity, adapting, perseverance, collaboration, and creativity.

Theory: The role of serendipity

The first theory of success that played a role in the creation of the minions was serendipity. The development of the minions had their origins in the birth of Christopher Meledandri in New York City in 1959. His parents adopted a child-rearing technique popular during the 1960s where parents treated their children like adults. As a result of this parenting approach, Meledandri never saw any cartoons or animated movies. Instead, his early film experiences came courtesy of Woody Allen, Stanley Kubrick and Martin Scorsese, rather than Walt Disney. According to

Meledandri, "the films that I was exposed to were the films my parents were interested in seeing as opposed to anything remotely resembling a film that was appropriate for children." Being raised by parents who incorporated this type of child-rearing strategy was completely serendipitous for Meledandri. Unfortunately, a month before graduating college, serendipity would strike again, this time tragically, as his father died of a heart attack. Meledandri had to attend to his father's affairs and phase out his business. The occurrence and development of events by chance, without any control or influence from Meledandri, played a critical role in his development.

Theory: Adapt

A second theory on success regarding the necessity of adaptation also played a role in the development of the minions. One of his father's friends, Dan Melnick, was a producer who had made films such as *All That Jazz* and *Straw Dogs*. He offered Mr. Meledandri a job as a gofer. Far from glamorous, his responsibilities included taking the dog to the vet, to go shopping for Christmas gifts, to being a courier for 35-mm film canisters so that [Melnick] could screen movies at his house. Yet the experience he gained was invaluable. Meledandri learned to adapt and opened himself up to learning as much as possible through the experience that so many others might have turned down or rejected since it was too mundane. Meledandri "gained access and exposure to virtually every aspect of producing a film, from the earliest conversations about ideas, to script development, to scheduling and budgeting, to marketing." Although he had experience in New York City, working in Hollywood required him to adapt. According to Meledandri, "I was coming from New York City so I thought I was pretty savvy but I found it quite intimidating, actually as I went from having studied Billy Wilder films in school to seeing Billy Wilder have lunch with my boss."

Theory: Perseverance

Meledandri also demonstrated another trait that researchers have identified as critical to achieving personal or professional success: perseverance. As he continued to gain increasing responsibility in Hollywood, Meledandri eventually worked on a major studio project entitled *Titan A.E.* that involved a mix of traditional animation with computer generated imagery (CGI). It was a rather embarrassing failure and was an extremely painful experience for him. Fortunately, his job was spared but he had to persevere through the failure and embarrassment. After his failure, he used Blue Sky Studios, a small New York-based company that had never produced anything longer than three minutes. The result was *Ice Age* and a string of other hits followed before he left in 2007 to start Illumination Entertainment, home of the minions, with the backing of Universal Pictures.

Theory: Collaboration

A fourth research theory highlighted in the success of the minions involves collaboration. Without his ability to collaborate, Meledandri would have never been able to bring the minions to life. The minions are products of Illumination Entertainment cofounded by Meledandri and Universal Pictures in 2007. A good deal of the minion animation was done in Paris, following the 2011 purchase of Mac Guff Ligne, a French digital studio, in a deal that was financed by Universal. Meledandri founded Illumination on the idea that his movies should be created by a group of people that have an international complexion. Renaud, for example, is French. According to Meledandri "we are trying to move away from the idea that these are American movies to be enjoyed by a global audience."

Theory: Creativity

A fifth trait that researchers have identified, creativity, is also prominent in the backstory of the minions. No one person created the minions. In fact, they were not event part of the first draft of the screenplay. According to co-screenwriter Cinco Paul "In the script, we just said, 'Gru's minions do this or do that' in the initial draft. And then, the film's directors, Pierre Coffin and Chris Renaud came up with the characters' design and the philosophical concept of the minions with their unintelligible voice and tic-tac shaped bodies." When creating the minions, Coffin and Renaud looked for inspiration from some of the silver screen's most notable toadies, particularly the Oompa Loompas from "Willy Wonka & the Chocolate Factory" (1971) and Jawas from "Star Wars: Episode IV – A New Hope" (1977). Creativity helped bring the minions to life.

Christopher Meledandri's ability to respond to serendipity, adapt to uncomfortable and new experiences, persevere difficult situations and failures, collaborate with others, and encourage an environment of creativity all contributed to the success of the minions. There was no one single situation that led to their creation. As with most successful ventures, it unfolded over time and involved a variety of steps along the way. The lesson from this analysis of the minion backstory is that the man who was never allowed to see children's movies grew up to become a leading producer of them. The backstory of Christopher Meledandri and the minions resembles that of many other successful people and ventures in that success was the byproduct of both intention and circumstance and there was no one specific path. Keep that in mind as you translate your vision into reality.

"No bird soars in a calm."

—Wilbur Wright

Endnotes

1. Viv Groskop, "'Shelf-help' Books Set to Fill Publishers' Coffers in 2014," *The Guardian*, December 28, 2013.
2. Ibid.
3. David Runciman, "Politics or Technology-Which Will Save the World?" *The Guardian*, May 23, 2014.
4. Thomas L. Friedman, "A Theory of Everything (Sort of)" *The New York Times*, August 13, 2011.
5. Ibid.
6. Dan Schawbel, "Geoff Colvin: Why Humans Will Triumph over Machines," *Forbes*, August 4, 2015.
7. Internet World Stats website: www.internetworldstats.com/top20 .htm (accessed July 2, 2015).
8. Donald Melanson, "UN: Worldwide Internet Users Hit Two Billion, Cellphone Subscriptions Top Five Billion," *Engadget*, January 28, 2011.
9. Andrew C. Revkin, "U.N.: Young and Old Boom on the Road to 9 Billion," *The New York Times*, March 11, 2009.
10. Carolynn Duffy Marsan, "10 Fool-proof Predictions for the Internet in 2020," *PC World*, January 5, 2010.
11. "IBM 2010 Global CEO Study," IBM Press release dated May 18, 2010.
12. Rose Eveleth, "Academics Write Papers Arguing over How Many People Read (and Cite) Their Papers," *Smithsonian Magazine*, March 25, 2014.
13. Daniel S. Hamermsesh, *Beauty Pays: Why Attractive People Are More Successful*, Princeton, NJ: Princeton University Press, 2011.
14. Henry William Chesbrough, *New Frontiers in Open Innovation*, New York City, NY: Oxford University Press, 2014.
15. Sian Beilock, "How Your Partner's Personality Impacts Your Career Success," *Psychology Today*, December 3, 2014.
16. Richard B. Gunderman, "Why Do Some People Succeed Where Others Fail? Implications for Education," *Radiology*, Vol. 226, 2002, pp. 29–31.

17. American Express, *The 2013 Life Twist Study*: An independent report commissioned by American Express.

18. Ibid.

19. Jacquelyn Smith, "This Is How Americans Define Success," *Business Insider*, October 3, 2014.

20. David Wallis, "Increasingly, Retirees Dump Their Possessions and Hit the Road," *The New York Times*, August 29, 2014; and Svati Kirsten Narula, "You Should Spend Money on Experiences, Not Things," *CityLab*, August 28, 2014.

21. Art Carey, "Taking the Measure of Happiness," *Philadelphia Inquirer*, June 2, 2013.

22. Seth Godin, *The Icarus Deception*, New York City, NY: Penguin, 2012.

23. For more information visit Paulo Coelho's website: www.paulocoelho.com/.

24. David Brooks, "Respect the Future," *The New York Times*, April 2, 2012.

25. Leslie Becker-Phelps, "Don't Just React: Choose Your Response," *Psychology Today*, July 23, 2013.

26. Craig Lambert, "The Psyche on Automatic," *Harvard Magazine*, November-December 2010.

27. David Brooks, "Matter Over Mind," *The New York Times*, April 20, 2011.

28. Craig Lambert, "The Psyche on Automatic," *Harvard Magazine*, November-December 2010.

29. *"Ted Talks: Most Viewed TED Talks". Retrieved 21 December 2015.*

30. Amy Cuddy, Presence: *Bringing Your Boldest Self to Your Biggest Challenges*, New York: Little, Brown and Company, 2015.

CHAPTER 1

Have a Bias Toward Action

Introduction

In a world where three billion people rely on advanced mobile technology and powerful computers to engage in real-time messaging, news reporting, and picture sharing, success is the one constant that still requires persistence. Any examination into success needs to recognize the preponderance of technology, its continual adaptation and its reach around the globe. Just because the technology we have today allows us to do things faster than our parents or grandparents does not mean there is such a thing as overnight success. Understanding there is no such thing as an overnight success is one of the most important stepping stones to use throughout life for personal growth and professional development. The idea of overnight success continues to exist as a prevalent cultural myth. It keeps many people from understanding and appreciating what it takes to build a meaningful career and establish purposeful influence.

As Jason Fried and David Heinemeier Hansson noted in their best-selling book *Rework*: "You know those overnight-success stories you've heard about? It's not the whole story. Dig deeper and you'll usually find people who have busted their asses for years to get into a position where things could take off."[1] Fried and Hansson concluded that slow, measured growth and patience are the two key traits a person needs because "you have to do it for a long time before the right people notice."[2] The pursuit of goals, regardless of size, requires constant commitment and unwavering persistence, especially in the face of obstacles and setbacks. "The best-kept secret in the startup world is that there is no such thing as an overnight success,"[3] wrote George Bradt, founder of executive onboarding group PrimeGenesis. Echoing the authors of *Rework*, Bradt observed that "success typically takes six to seven years–if you survive the first three."[4]

Grinding work out over an extended period of time with the intention of making adjustments in order to keep moving forward requires a high level of self-awareness coupled with what researchers have labeled grit.

MacArthur Fellow Angela Duckworth, a psychology professor at the University of Pennsylvania, identified this grinding out as grit—the tendency to sustain interest in and effort toward very long-term goals and equips individuals to pursue, especially challenging aims over years and even decades.[5] Duckworth noted that people who "accomplished great things often combined a passion for a single mission with an unswerving dedication to achieve that mission, whatever the obstacles and however long it might take."[6] Duckworth recognizes that the essence of grit remains elusive as it has hundreds of correlates, with nuances and anomalies that include, but are not limited to the following characteristics: courage, conscientiousness, follow-through, resilience, and the pursuit of excellence not perfection.[7] The field of publishing is a good case study of authors who have had to practice resilience in order to get their work published.

Throughout history authors have had to demonstrate grit amidst multiple rejections by publishers. The reach and frequency of rejections is so common of a phenomenon that there is a website dedicated to bestsellers that were initially rejected - litrejections.com.[8] "The halls of the literary establishment echo with tales of now-revered writers who initially faced failure."[9] Stephen King is just one example whose *Carrie* was rejected 30 times before being published. In 1973, before *Carrie* was published, King, his wife Tabby, and their toddler and newborn lived in a doublewide trailer. King drove a rust-bucket Buick held together with baling wire and duct tape. King's wife, Tabby, worked second-shift at Dunkin' Donuts while he taught English at a private high school.[10] King also worked summers at an industrial laundry and moonlighted as a janitor and gas pump attendant. Dealing with constant rejection and criticism from publishers and readers from the articles he did get published in the nudie mag market, King grew frustrated at his writing. He even through a draft of *Carrie* out in the trash but Tabby found it and told him to continue writing. They both had a bias towards action. With that King finished his first novel and after 30 rejections sold it to Doubleday.[11]

There is a caveat, however, to this bias towards action with a reliance on grit; the action steps one takes need to be focused on a specific goal and not just busy work. It is easy to be busy. It is far more difficult to practice the trait of grit. All too often people obsess over how busy they are without any sense of accomplishment. Researchers have recently examined "idleness aversion and the need for justifiable busyness."[12] Some people are busy just for the sake of being busy. These people are not grinding it out nor are they working towards a specific goal or translating theory into action. They are merely justifying how busy they are. Be careful not to fall into the busyness trap. As Tim Kreider wrote in a *New York Times* editorial people who have self-imposed a label of 'always busy' on themselves do so out of their addiction to busyness itself and dread what they might have to face in its absence."[13] *Grinding it out for long periods of time require one to have a bias toward action and often involves engaging in deliberate practice, demonstrating the characteristics of a maverick, and exhibiting courageous behavior.*

Engage in Deliberate Practice

Two books that specifically examine the theory of deliberate practice are Malcolm Gladwell's *Outliers: The Story of Success* and Geoff Colvin's *Talent is Over-rated: What Really Separates World-Class Performers from Everybody Else.* Both books examine how individuals achieved world-class mastery that put them at the top of their field. Gladwell's chapter entitled "The 10,000 Hour Rule" identified that world-class performers, The Beatles, for example, spent approximately 10,000 hours working at their specialty to arrive at the top. These were not overnight successes or people who merely exploited natural talent. Rather, they spent years focused on perfecting one thing. Colvin further supports Gladwell's point and states three very important conclusions. First, "everyone who has achieved exceptional performance has encountered terrible difficulties along the way. There are no exceptions."[14] Second, "what the evidence shouts most loudly is striking, liberating news that great performance is not reserved for a preordained few. It is available to you and to everyone."[15] Colvin also concluded that talent, IQ, and experience, once thought to be the three pillars of success, play a less important role than previously thought when compared to one's drive, decisiveness, and grit.

Both authors believe that "great performance is available to you and to everyone." Deliberate practice research indicates that long-term success requires a minimum of 10 years of engagement, coupled with grit, or the ability to persevere difficult situations and a willingness to adapt to challenges as they arise. Larry Bird's career as a basketball superstar is a case study in deliberate practice. Bird settled on basketball as his primary sport in high school. When he realized he might excel in the sport, he began to practice day and night. "I played when I was cold and my body was aching and I was so tired," he told *Sports Illustrated*. "I don't know why, I just kept playing and playing . . . . I guess I always wanted to make the most out of it."[16] He also thrived on learning and playing with people who were better than him from such a young age. That attitude would be one of the key ingredients to his long-term success. Bird started for French Lick/ West Baden's high school team, Springs Valley High School, where he left as the school's all-time scoring leader.

Following a sophomore season that was shortened by a broken ankle, Bird emerged as a star during his junior year. Springs Valley went 19-2 and young Larry became a local celebrity. Fans always seemed to be willing to give a ride to Bird's parents, who couldn't afford a car of their own. As a senior, Bird became the school's all-time scoring champion and about 4,000 people attended his final home game. Bird's high school coach, Jim Jones, was a key factor to his success. "Jonesie," as Bird called him, would help Bird and his friends practice any day of the week. Bird would demonstrate deliberate practice by often going to the gym early, shooting between classes, and staying late into the evening. It was during this time that he played with the older students working at a nearby hotel.[17]

Bird received a scholarship to play college basketball for Bob Knight and the Indiana University Hoosiers in 1974. However, he was overwhelmed by the size of the campus and number of students and was not mentally ready for this stage of life; according to Bird, "It didn't take long to realize that I was out of my cocoon." He dropped out of Indiana after 24 days, disappointing his mother. Bird returned home to French Lick where he enrolled in the nearby Northwood Institute before dropping out. He had a short marriage that ended in divorce. To support himself and his daughter from that marriage, he took a job with the City Department of French Lick. He drove a garbage truck and helped pick up trash and to maintain parks and roads in the district. During this time, he also played AAU basketball for Hancock Construction.[18]

Bird faced personal loss during the same period when his father committed suicide. After that tragic event, he decided to return to college.[19] This time he went to Indiana State in Terre Haute, where he was coached by Bob King. He had little confidence in his academic abilities, but felt that he could help the basketball team, the Sycamores. By that time he had grown another two inches. He was 6 feet 9 inches and 220 pounds. Bird had to sit out his first season at Indiana State because of rules having to do with players moving from one school to another. That year, the Sycamores went 13–12 (won 13 games and lost 12). When he was allowed to play in the 1976–77 season, his first year on the team, the same Sycamores earned a 25–3 record—their best in almost 30 years.

When he was at Indiana State, Bird became the most talked about college player in the country. He always played with and for the team and always shared his fame with his fellow players both on and off the court. The Boston Celtics drafted Bird in 1978. He had the option of playing professional basketball right away, but he chose to stay in school and finish his degree. The Celtics worked out a deal for Bird after his graduation. The contract signed on June 8, 1979, gave Bird $650,000 per year for five years, a total of $3.25 million.[20] This sum was a record for a rookie in any sport. The Boston fans made no secret of their expectations for their new headliner. Bird did not disappoint them and would eventually go on to win several championships with the Celtics. Bird had a bias toward action and engaged in deliberate practice for years to achieve greatness on the basketball court. Those who have a bias toward action are often considered mavericks.

Demonstrate the Characteristics of a Maverick

Just because something has never been done before doesn't mean it cannot be done. This is the fundamental belief of being a maverick. Mavericks often possess the perfect blend of self-delusions and ego to succeed, whereas others either failed or dare not go. The latest research on being a maverick comes from Elliroma Gardner, an organizational psychologist at the London School of Economics and Political Science. Gardner coined the term maverickism as a continuum where people fall along a range. Some people are likely to be high in maverickism, others moderate, and some low. By constructing this scale, Gardner is able to better quantitatively measure maverick tendencies.[21] Bill Gates, Steve Jobs, Steve Wozniak, Sergey Brin, and Larry Page are often described as mavericks.[22] With her maverickism scale, however, Gardner's research indicates that being creative, taking risks, breaking rules, and being goal focused are traits many people actually have but they don't always have the same scale of results as Jobs and the others, which makes them less well-known.[23] If one is open to new experiences, relentlessly curious and maintains a fascination with the world and a compulsion to understand how it works, then it is possible to be a maverick on a smaller scale. This is important to realize because an individual translating their thoughts into action might hold Steve Jobs up as the large-scale maverick to emulate. In actuality, all one needs to do is to recognize that the pursuit of one's dream, and its impact on making a difference in this world, no matter how small, demonstrates maverick behavior. In some historical examples, a few mavericks started out on a small scale and then evolved over time. The Impressionists artists in 19th-century Paris are one such example.

The Impressionists were radicals for their sketchy, light-filled paintings and for the fact that they established their own exhibition—apart from the annual salon. In 19th-century France, a jury chose the artists who could exhibit their work in the salon. Claude Monet, August Renoir, Edgar Degas, Berthe Morisot, Alfred Sisley, and several other artists, chose to demonstrate maverick behavior and went against tradition. They decided that they did not want to, nor could they afford to, wait for the jury to approve of their art. They all had experienced rejection by the salon jury and refused to wait a year in between exhibitions and wanted to sell their art to earn some much needed income. So, in an attempt to get recognized outside of the official channel of the salon, these artists banded together and held their own exhibition.[24]

They pooled their money, rented a studio that belonged to the famous photographer Nadar and set a date for their first exhibition together. They called themselves the Anonymous Society of Painters, Sculptors, and Printmakers.[25] The Impressionists held eight exhibitions from 1874 to 1886. The first exhibition did not repay them monetarily, but it drew the critics who decided their art was abominable since it wasn't finished. They called it "just impressions." The public, at first hostile, gradually came to believe that the maverick Impressionists had captured a fresh and original vision, even if the art critics and art establishment disapproved of the new style.[26] While the Impressionists were mavericks in the world of art, Starbucks CEO Howard Shultz and Chick-fil-A founder S. Truett Cathy exhibited the perfect blend of self-delusion and ego to succeed in business.

When he wanted to open up the first Starbucks in Japan, CEO Schultz had to challenge the status quo. In 1996, Starbucks was advised by a blue-chip consulting company that opening in Japan would be problematic because of many reasons, among which included the high price of real estate, a nonsmoking policy in stores, and a cultural concern that no Japanese consumer would want to be seen carrying anything to eat or drink while walking around outside.[27] Since 80 percent of Starbucks' business back then was classified as "to go," this last concern was particularly distressing. Even though no one at Starbucks had any international experience, and against the conclusions reached by the consultants, Schultz challenged the status quo and opened the first Starbucks in Japan. On opening day marked by high humidity and with CNN cameras covering the opening, hundreds of young Japanese people waited to enter the store after Schultz cut the ribbon. Without advertising and with the Internet in its infancy, how could news about the Starbucks brand travel around the world in 1996? For Schultz, challenging the status quo was built upon the foundation that Starbucks had become a company that people were proud to support and a cup they were proud to hold. In the early 1990s, Starbucks become the first company in America to offer comprehensive health insurance to every employee, even those working part-time. When it went public on June 26, 1992, some observers expressed concern that this type of health-care policy would dilute shareholder value. For Shultz, however, his policy helped reduce the high cost of attrition if you treated people with respect and dignity.[28]

Like Schultz, S. Truett Cathy challenged the status quo when he opened his first Chick-fil-A store in Atlanta's Greenbriar Mall in 1967.

True to his Christian business practices, Cathy told mall management that his store had to be closed on Sunday. For over 20 years, Cathy had taught Sunday school and never opened his other restaurant, The Dwarf Grill on a Sunday and wanted to continue the tradition. Amidst protests from the mall management that told him Sunday would be his busiest day, Cathy challenged the status quo and stayed true to his principles. To this day, Chick-fil-A restaurants are still closed on Sunday.[29] In true maverick form Truett noted that "we should ask ourselves what's important and what's not important. When you live by your convictions, people respect that. It's important to be consistent in living your convictions."[30] With a bias toward action, Shultz and Truett were mavericks that sparked a revolution in their respective industries. Facing one issue after another, both individuals also had to demonstrate courage throughout their life.

Exhibit Courage

Aristotle believed courage to be the most important quality in a man when he declared "courage is the first of human virtues because it makes all others possible." Recent research into understanding what courage is and how we might be able to cultivate the ability to exhibit it when necessary is providing new insight into having a bias toward action. Uri Nili and Yadin Dudai from the Weizmann Institute of Science in Rehovot, Israel recently determined just how courage works in the brain, finding that a region called the subgenual anterior cingulate cortex (sgACC) is the driving force behind courageous acts.[31] Generally speaking, there are many forms of courage but the four most common are physical, collective, moral, and intellectual. Physical courage is a willingness to push the limits of one's body; collective courage refers to when one joins or leads other like-minded individuals; moral courage is the courage to stand up for one's beliefs in the face of overwhelming opposition and intellectual courage is the willingness to come out in favor of an idea that others find ridiculous. The etymology of courage comes from Latin *cor* meaning "from the heart." Having heart is often the deciding factor between those who translate their dreams into reality and other who just dream.

Valentino Achak Deng, Ben Hogan, and Roger Bannister each exemplify different forms of courage.

Growing up in a remote Sudanese town, Deng was caught up in his country's civil war. Separated from his friends and family, Deng became one of the 27,000 "lost boys" of Sudan who were displaced and/or orphaned during war where an unimaginable two million people died. His family lost to the civil war, Deng had the courage to find a refugee camp where he learned to read and write.[32] After a while he was accepted as a refugee into the United States, settled in Atlanta, GA, and met author Dave Eggers who spent the next three years writing *What Is The What: The Autobiography of Valentino Achak Deng: A Novel*. When the book was published in 2006, Deng established the Valentino Achak Deng Foundation. All proceeds from the book support Valentino's Foundation. The Foundation's first major project is the construction of an educational center in Valentino's hometown of Marial Bai. The Marial Bai Secondary School is the first high school in the entire region, where decades of war completely devastated the educational system.[33] While Deng used his courage to return home, Hogan used his courage to succeed despite three personal tragedies.

American professional golfer Ben Hogan, one of the greatest players in the history of the game, is notable for his profound influence on the golf swing theory and his legendary ball-striking ability. He practiced and achieved great success amidst many personal tragedies. First, his father committed suicide when Hogan was nine years old, which left an impact on him forever. His father's suicide placed the Hogan family in financial difficulties, so his mother moved them from their rural Texas home to Fort Worth. To make ends meet, Hogan took to caddying to make money, and golf became his road out of poverty. Second, it took Hogan 10 years to win his first professional tournament during which time he went broke more than once. Hogan practiced until his palms were cracked and blistered, then soaked his hands in pickle brine to toughen them up, and practiced some more.[34] Finally, he needed 59 days in the hospital to recover from a near death car accident that left Hogan with a double fracture of the pelvis, a fractured collar bone, and near-fatal blood clots.[35] With courage and perseverance, Hogan demonstrated time and

Progression of Mile Record Time, 1865–1999

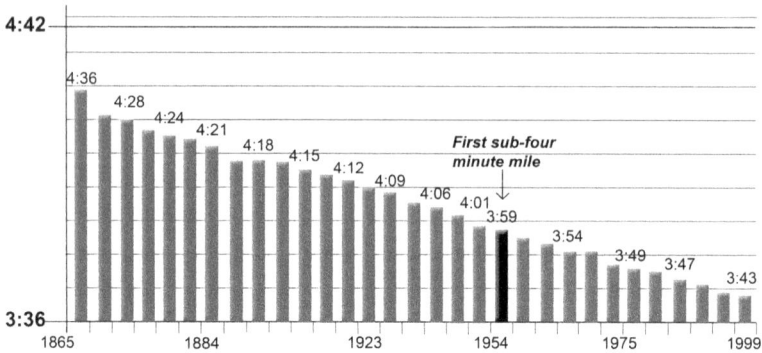

again that despite a personal tragedy, a decade's worth of struggle and a near death experience success is still possible.

Successful people know that just because it hasn't been done before doesn't mean it cannot be done. Roger Bannister and the sub-4 minute mile is a perfect case study. Prior to 1954, many people believed that 4 minutes was a physical barrier that no runner could break. On May 6, 1954, Roger Bannister had convinced himself that he could break that barrier and his effort proved successful. On that day, not succumbing to the idea that it was impossible, he ran the mile in 3 minutes, 59.4 seconds. It is also fascinating to examine what happened after Roger Bannister broke the 4-minute mile. Fifty-six days later, John Landy ran the 4-minute mile in 3 minutes and 57.9 seconds in Finland. Bannister and Landy would race each other in the Mile of the Century where Bannister won in 3 minutes and 58.8 seconds. Within three years, by the end of 1957, 16 other runners also cracked the 4-minute mile. The breaking of the 4-minute mile was so significant that *Forbes* names it as one of the greatest athletic achievements of all time.[36] Bannister had the courage to do something that no other person was able to do physically. Doing so proved to others that the impossible was indeed possible. Hicham El Guerrouj (Morocco) is the current men's record holder with his time of 3:43.13, while Svetlana Masterkova (Russia) has the women's record of 4:12.56.[37]

Conclusion

Jack Welch, former CEO of General Electric, wrote, "In real life, strategy is actually very straightforward. You pick a general direction and implement like crazy." Herb Kelleher of Southwest Airlines famously remarked, "We have a 'strategic plan.' It's called doing things."[38] Doing things and having a bias toward action might mean you have to move forward without knowing all the answers. Taking action means you often find yourself in unchartered territory. Successful people know that they do not have to have all of the answers. Tim Brown, CEO of the Palo Alto design firm IDEO, said, "I know I don't have all the answers . . . nobody does. I'm personally perfectly comfortable admitting that I don't know the answers and that I am more interested in the questions anyway."[39] Successful people have a bias toward action by engaging in deliberate practice, demonstrating the characteristics of a maverick, and exhibiting courageous behavior. Their lives are built upon the foundation of action and that approach allows them to translate their dreams into reality. This bias toward action characteristic was summed up nicely by Will Smith: "You might have more talent than me, you might be smarter than me, you might be sexier than me, you might be all of those things—you got it on me in nine categories. But if we get on the treadmill together you're getting off first, or I'm going to die. It's really that simple."[40]

Questions and Resources for Characteristic#1: Have a bias toward action

Reading list

- Malcolm Gladwell, *Outliers: The Story of Success*
- Geoff Colvin, *Talent is Over-rated: What Really Separates World-Class Performers from Everybody Else*
- Daniel H. Pink*, Drive: The Surprising Truth About What Motivates Us*
- Ken Robinson, *The Element: How Finding Your Passion Changes Everything*
- Elliroma Gardiner and CJ Jackson, "Workplace mavericks: how personality and risk-taking propensity predicts maverickism." *British Journal of Psychology*, November 2012.
- Howard Schultz and Joanne Gordon, *Onward: How Starbucks Fought for Its Life without Losing Its Soul*
- Sue Roe, *The Private Lives of the Impressionists*
- S. Truett Cathy, *How Did You Do It, Truett?*
- Cynthia L. S. Pury and Shane J. Lopez, editors. *The Psychology of Courage: Modern Research on an Ancient Virtue*

Videos

- Angela Lee Duckworth, *The key to success? Grit*, TED Talk, April 2013
- Richard St. John, *8 secrets of success*, TED Talk, February 2005

Questions

- Are you busy just for the sake of being busy?
- How often do you say "I am so busy?" Why do you even say it in the first place?
- Why do you think most people will avoid deliberate practice?
- What role does goal setting have in deliberate practice?
- Have you dedicated 10,000 hours to one activity?

- Do you believe that you can achieve success with deliberate practice?
- What role does self-discipline play in the engagement of deliberate practice?
- Have you ever worked for a maverick? If so, what qualities did they demonstrate?
- Why are mavericks so often misunderstood?
- What might people perceive mavericks as threatening?
- Do you have any of the following characteristics of a maverick:
    i. Openness
    ii. Creativity
    iii. Willingness to take risks
    iv. Big picture oriented
    v. Unafraid to break rules
    vi. Perseverance
- How often do you demonstrate courage?
- Have you admired individuals for their courage?
- What holds people back from being courageous?
- Where could you use a bit more courage in your life?
- Have you helped anyone advance their courage?
- Do you have a bias toward action?
- Are you willing to engage in deliberate practice, demonstrate the characteristics of a maverick, or exhibit courageous behavior?
- Have you thought about how hard you are working towards a goal?

Exercises

True Grit Assessment: Psychologists at the University of Pennsylvania, University of Michigan, and West Point developed a Grit Scale, presented in *The Intelligent Optimist* (November 2012) to test their hypothesis that persistence was as important to success as intelligence. To measure your own grit, answer the following questions with A meaning very much like me, B mostly like me, C somewhat like me, D not much like me, and E not like me at all:

1. I have overcome setbacks to conquer an important challenge.
2. New ideas and projects sometimes distract me from previous ones.
3. My interests change from year to year.
4. Setbacks don't discourage me.
5. I have been obsessed with a certain idea for a short time, but later lost interest.
6. I am a hard worker.
7. I often set a goal, but later choose to pursue a different one.
8. I have difficulty maintaining focus on projects that take several months to complete.
9. I finish whatever I began.
10. I have achieved a goal that took years of work.
11. I become interested in new pursuits every few months.
12. I am diligent.

Determine your grit score: For questions 1, 4, 6, 9, 10, and 12 assign the following points: a = 5, b = 4, c = 3, d = 2, e = 1. For questions 2, 3, 5, 7, 8, and 11 assign the following points: a = 1, b = 2, c = 3, d = 4, e = 5. Now, add all your points and divide by 12. The maximum score is 5 (meaning you are extremely gritty) and the lowest is 1 (you have no grit at all).

How Good Do You Want To Be? Assessment

Objective: To challenge you to think about the level of performance you want to achieve during your lifetime.

Directions: All you have to do is answer one question: "So how good do you want to be?" Only you can answer this question. Take your time. Do some research and figure out if you want to be quite good, the best in the world, or somewhere in between. Like most of the assessments, your answer to this question will probably change over time.

SO HOW GOOD
DO YOU WANT TO BE?

QUITE GOOD   GOOD   VERY GOOD   THE BEST IN YOUR FIELD   THE BEST IN THE WORLD

Time is what we want most, but what we use worst.

—William Penn

Endnotes

1. Jason Fried and David Hansson, *Rework*, New York, Random House, 2010, p. 196.
2. Ibid.
3. George Bradt, "Why Overnight Start-up Success Is A Myth," *Forbes*, October 23, 2013.
4. Ibid.
5. Rieva Lesonsky, "Is True Grit the Most Important Factor to Success?" *American Express Open Forum*, April 21, 2014.
6. Paul Tough, "What if the Secret to Success Is Failure?" *The New York Times Magazine*, September 14, 2011.
7. Margaret M. Perlis, "5 Characteristics of Grit-How Many Do You Have?" *Forbes*, October 29, 2013.
8. Kavita Das, "Writers Shouldn't Romanticize Rejection," *The Atlantic*, November 7, 2015.
9. Ibid.
10. Lucas Reilly, "How Stephen King's Wife Saved 'Carrie' and Launched His Career," *Mental Floss,* October 17, 2003.
11. Ibid.
12. Christopher K. Hsee, et al., "Idleness Aversion and the Need for Justifiable Busyness," *Psychological Science*, July 2010.
13. Tim Kreider, "The 'Busy' Trap," *The New York Times,* June 30, 2012.
14. Geoff Colvin, *Talent is Overrated: What Really Separates World-Class Performers from Everybody Else*, New York: Portfolio, 2008.
15. Geoff Colvin, *Talent is Overrated: What Really Separates World-Class Performers from Everybody Else*, New York: Portfolio, 2008.
16. Seth Davis, "*When March Went Mad: The Game That Transformed Basketball,* Times Books: New York City, NY 2009.
17. Wikipedia, "Larry Bird," accessed November 10, 2015.
18. Ibid.
19. Larry Schwartz, "Plain and simple, Bird one of the best," *ESPN.com*, no date.
20. Encyclopedia of World Biography, "Larry Bird," accessed December 1, 2015.
21. "Seems Awkward, Ignores the Rules, but Brilliant: Meet the Maverick Job Candidate," *TIME Magazine*, August 29, 2012.

22. For more information see: Devin D. Johnson, "Be a Maverick," *The Entrepreneur Mind,* 2013.

23. William C. Taylor, *Mavericks at Work: Why the Most Original Minds in Business Win*, New York, Harper Paperback, 2008.

24. Impressionism: Art and Modernity, www.metmuseum.org/toah/hd/imml/hd_imml.htm.

25. Ibid.

26. A detailed story on the Impressionists can be found in Malcom Gladwell, *David and Goliath: Underdogs, Misfits, and the Art of Battling Giants*, New York, Little, Brown & Co., 2013.

27. "How Starbucks Built a Global Brand, UCLA" video located at www.youtube.com/watch?v=_kAiEO6jP48.

28. Ibid.

29. Truett Cathy, *How Did You Do It, Truett?: A Recipe for Success*, Looking Glass Books, Inc.: Decatur, Georgia, 2007.

30. Ibid.

31. Daniela Schiller, "Snakes in the MIR Machine: A Study of Courage, *Scientific American*, July 20, 2010.

32. Nicholas Kristof, "His Gift Changes Lives," *The New York Times*, December 16, 2009.

33. Ibid.

34. Thane Peterson, "The Hard Life of a Golfing Great," *Businessweek*, June 17, 2004.

35. Damon Hack, "Hogan's Return: Back From Tragedy to Win the 1950 U.S. Open," *Golf*, June 24, 2010.

36. David M. Ewalt Lacey Rose, "The Greatest Individual Athletic Achievements," *Forbes*, January 29, 2008.

37. "Mile run world record progression," *Wikipedia*, accessed December 2, 2015.

38. Ben Casnocha, *My Start Up Life: What a (Very) Young CEO Learned on His Journey Through Silicon Valley*, John Wiley & Sons, Inc. New York City, NY, 2007.

39. Adam Bryant, "He Prizes Questions More Than Answers," *The New York Times* interview with Tim Brown, October 24, 2009.

40. Will Smith interview on Tavis Smiley, YouTube uploaded January 3, 2008, www.youtube.com/watch?v=M88uMRwsj0U.

CHAPTER 2

Engage with Others

Introduction

The history of successful people and ventures is filled with stories involving collaboration.[1] Successful collaborators do more than just work together. According to Michael Schrage "successful collaborators work together in a shared physical, virtual, or digital space where they agree to jointly create, manipulate, iterate, capture and critique the representations of the reality they seek to discover or design."[2] This holds true for collaboration around products, processes, services, songs, or the exploration of scientific principles. Shared space is the essential means, medium, and mechanism that makes collaboration possible. The efforts of Orville and Wilbur Wright as well as Art Fry and Spencer Silver are just two of the many success stories built upon a foundation of collaboration.

In 1878, Wright's father gave them a toy helicopter with twirling blades powered by a rubber band. This toy sparked their interest in flight. After designing and building a printing press, the brothers opened a bicycle shop in Dayton, Ohio. By 1896, the pair had manufactured their own brand of bicycles and turned their attention toward flight. Between 1900 and 1902, the brothers experimented with kites, gliders, and a wind tunnel and on December 17, 1903 flew the first successful heavier-than-air powered aircraft near Kill Devil Hills, about four miles south of Kitty Hawk, North Carolina.[3] Two years later, the brothers built a plane capable of sustaining flight longer than half an hour. In 1909, the Wrights had incorporated the Wright Co., which continued to develop and sell increasingly sophisticated aircraft until their deaths. Throughout their work on the airplane, the Wright brothers pioneered wind tunnel designs and tests as shared space for flight design where they could collaborate with each other as well as those interested in supporting their vision.[4]

Engagement with others through collaboration also contributed to the creation and success of the post-it note.

In 1968, while working at 3M trying to create a super strong adhesives for the aerospace industry, Spencer Silver accidentally managed to create an incredibly weak, pressure-sensitive adhesive agent called Acrylate Copolymer Microspheres that could easily be peeled off of a surface and it was also reusable. Since 3M management viewed Silver's creation as too weak to be useful, the discovery was a dead end. Silver spent the next five years trying to figure out a way to use his discovery.[5] Finally, in 1973, when Geoff Nicholson was made products laboratory manager at 3M, Silver approached him immediately and suggested 3M create a bulletin board without the need for tape or tacks since the paper could easily be removed from the board. While that idea gained little traction, luck would play a role when 3M product development engineer Art Fry attended one of Silver's seminars on the low-tack adhesive.

Fry sung in a church choir in St. Paul, Minnesota and had a problem of accidentally losing his song page markers in his hymn book while singing. From this, he eventually had the stroke of genius to use some of Silver's adhesive to help keep the slips of paper in the hymnal. Fry then suggested to Nicholson and Silver that they were using the adhesive backward. Instead of sticking the adhesive to the bulletin board, they should "put it on a piece of paper and then we can stick it to anything."[6] The original notes' yellow color was chosen by accident, as the lab next-door to the post-it team had only yellow scrap paper to use. 3M launched the product as "Press 'n Peel" in stores in four cities in 1977, but results were disappointing. A year later, 3M instead issued free samples directly to consumers in Boise, ID, with 94 percent of those who tried them indicating they would buy the product.[7] On April 6, 1980, "Press 'n Peel" was reintroduced in US stores as "post-it notes." The following year, they were launched in Canada and Europe. The partnership of Fry and Silver illustrate the collaborative culture fostered at 3M as well as their shared space for inventing a new adhesive application.

The ability of the Wright Brothers to pioneer flight and the efforts of Art Fry and Spencer Silver to bring a new adhesive application to market both illustrate the power of collaboration. By engaging with people outside of their normal circles, what researchers today label an open network, the inventors of the airplane and post-it note found new ways to engage with others. Thanks to the technological advancements available today, the power of collaboration has risen to an entirely new level. *Successful people engage with others and rely on collaboration efforts, have learned to leverage crowds, and intentionally live and work in open networks.*

Collaborate

Successful people rely on their ability to engage in planned as well as unplanned opportunities of collaboration. Paul W. Mattessich, Marta Murray-Close, and Barbara R. Monsey co-author a leading text in the field entitled *Collaboration: What Makes It Work, 2nd Edition: A Review of Research Literature on Factors Influencing Successful Collaboration*. They include a list of 20 factors that have repeatedly proven to have influence on the potential success of collaboration between multiple organizations known as The Wilder Collaboration Factors.[8] A few examples of the 20 factors and statements include:

- *Factor*: History of collaboration or cooperation in the community
  - ◦ *Statement*: Agencies in our community have a history of working together
  - ◦ *Statement*: Trying to solve problems through collaboration has been common in this community.
- *Factor*: Collaborative group seen as a legitimate leader in the community
  - ◦ *Statement*: Leaders in this community who are not part of our collaborative group seem hopeful about what we can accomplish
  - ◦ *Statement*: Others in this community who are not part of this collaboration would generally agree that the organizations involved in this collaborative project are the "right" organizations to make this work.

Excellent research on the power of collaboration is also found in Keith Sawyer's *Group Genius: The Creative Power of Collaboration*. Sawyer found that innovation is often the result of collaboration among disparate groups of people, not the lone genius so often portrayed in stories. Collaboration often drives creativity because innovation generally emerges from a series of events over time. Sawyer found five key ingredients to successful collaboration:

1. *Execution over preparation* The most innovative teams spent less time in the planning stage and more time executing. They improvised instead of planned.
2. *After the fact* Innovation emerges from the bottom up and is often unpredictable; and it's often only after the innovation has occurred that everyone realizes what's happened.
3. *Identifying new problems* The most creative groups are good at finding new problems rather than simply solving old ones.
4. *Diversity drives innovation* Groups are most effective when they are composed of people who have a variety of skills, knowledge, and perspective.
5. *Culture provides foundation* New technology helps, but it won't make an organization collaborative without the right culture and values in place.

Tracing the development of Wikipedia and the invisible bicycle helmet provide case studies of successful collaboration that resulted in two very innovative products.

Jimmy Wales was born in Huntsville, Alabama and earned his bachelor's and master's degrees in finance from Auburn University and the University of Alabama, respectively. While in graduate school, he taught at two universities, but left before completing a PhD to take a job in finance and later worked as the research director of a Chicago futures and options firm.[9] During his college years, he first learned of the potential of large-scale online collaboration when he became familiar with a type of virtual role playing game called Multi-User Dungeons (MUDs). In 1996, he founded the web portal Bomis, a male-oriented web portal featuring entertainment and adult content, with two partners. Although Bomis struggled to make money, it did provide him with the funding he needed to pursue his idea for an online encyclopedia. In March 2000, along with Larry Sanger, Wales launched a peer-reviewed, open-content encyclopedia called Nupedia. Nupedia was to have expert-written entries on a variety of topics and attract enough viewers that would allow advertising to be placed alongside the entries. Due to an arduous peer-review process, however, Nupedia failed to achieve any level of growth and published just 24 articles.

To help facilitate its growth and simplify the submission process, Wales and Sanger implemented a new tool called a wiki that programmer Ben Kovitz introduced to them in January 2001. This new tool would revolutionize the level of collaboration possible for anyone with Internet access around the globe. When Nupedia's experts rejected the wiki for fear that mixing amateur content with professionally researched material would compromise the integrity of Nupedia's information and damage the credibility, Wales and Sanger labeled the new project "Wikipedia" and went live on its own domain five days after its creation. In a 2006 TED talk Wales said that Wikipedia began with a very radical idea and that was for "all of us to imagine a world in which every single person on the planet is given free access to the sum of all human knowledge."[10] Since Wikipedia allowed anyone with Internet access to edit the site, the sum of all human knowledge could now be recorded on a more detailed level than previously thought possible. As an innovative global collaboration platform Wikipedia now has over 290 editions with the English Wikipedia having the largest collection of articles reaching 5 million in November 2015. There is a grand total, including all Wikipedias, of over 37 million articles in over 250 different languages. As of February 2014, it had 18 billion page views and nearly 500 million unique visitors each month.[11] The collaborative effort building the sum of all human knowledge is just one example of a successful venture born out of modern day collaboration efforts. The invisible bicycle helmet is another.

A pair of Swedish inventors, Anna Haupt and Terese Alstin designed the invisible bicycle helmet known as the Hövding over the course of eight years. The Hövding is also known as the world's first airbag bicycle helmet as it is stored in a decorative pouch worn around a rider's neck. When a rider crashes, a helium canister inflates the nylon hood within milliseconds. Hövding started out in 2005 as a master's thesis by the two founders who were studying Industrial Design at the University of Lund.

Haupt and Alstin had the idea of developing a new type of cycle helmet in response to the introduction of a law on mandatory helmet use for children up to the age of 15 in Sweden. The law triggered a debate on whether cycle helmets should be mandatory for adults. To design their invisible helmet, Haupt and Alstin collaborated with a variety of experts in various fields to create an innovative set of sensors that trigger the helmet to inflate out of its pouch upon a bicycle's impact. They added sensors to the Hövding that analyzed movement patterns 200 times a second to know when the rider is in a real crash.

To perfect the sensors, the two women simulated icy roads, car collisions, and other causes of crashes. Normal movements made by riders won't trigger the Hövding. Because the device stays inflated for several seconds, the head can sustain multiple impacts without damage. It also covers more of the face and neck while still allowing the wearer to see. In 2006, Hövding won the Venture Cup, after which Hövding Sweden AB was founded. Haupt said, "We don't like, as designers, to have this attitude that it's people who need to change, instead of the product that needs to change. And that's why we decided to see if we could improve them." By creating a whole new mind, they succeeded in creating a solution to the vanity aspect of wearing bicycle helmets. People want a product that leaves their hair intact. Their understanding of this vanity aspect helped the two innovators realize they "needed to really think new if we wanted to solve the problem."[12] While Haupt and Alstin designed the Hövding through intention sometimes collaboration happens through luck.

Some individuals define luck as the intersection of where preparation meets opportunity. To explore this question scientifically experimental psychologist, Max Gunter published *The Luck Factor: Why Some People Are Luckier Than Others and How You Can Become One of Them*. In his 1977 publication, Gunter identified five traits of lucky people:

- *The spider web structure*: network with others
- *The hunching skill*: believe that it is possible to perceive more than you see
- *The 'audentes fortuna juvat' (fortune favors the brave) phenomenon:* the lucky life is a zigzag, not a straight line.
- *The ratchet effect*: prevent bad luck from becoming worse luck.

- *The pessimism paradox*: lucky people often cultivate hard, dark pessimism as an essential item of survival equipment.

Recent investigations into luck have come from Professor Richard Wiseman of the University of Hertfordshire in England where he created a "luck lab." Wiseman measured five personality traits: agreeableness, conscientiousness, extroversion, neuroticism, and openness.[13] He discovered no differences between lucky and unlucky people on agreeableness and conscientiousness but did find significant differences for extroversion, neuroticism, and openness. After three years of intensive interviews and experiments with over 400 volunteers, Wiseman arrived at an astonishing conclusion: Luck is something that can be learned. It is available to anyone willing to pay attention to what he labeled the Four Essential Principles in his book *The Luck Factor*: creating chance opportunities, thinking lucky, feeling lucky, and denying fate. For example, "lucky people expect good things to happen, and when they do they embrace them. But even in the face of adversity, lucky people turn bad breaks into good fortune."[14] English theoretical physicist Stephen W. Hawking is one example. Although he is one of the longest ALS sufferers in history, Hawking wrote, "I was lucky to have chosen to work in theoretical physics, because that was one of the few areas in which my condition would not be a serious handicap."[15] Brian Glazer's remarkable career in Hollywood started out from a lucky situation and serves as just one example of a life where luck contributed to a successful life.

After graduating from the University of Southern California's School of Cinema-Television in 1974, Brian Glazer overheard a conversation between two men outside his apartment window one afternoon. One man was telling another how he had just quit a law clerk position for Peter Knecht at Warner Bros. Glazer needed a job that summer before he started USC Law School, so he called 411 to locate the phone number and called Knecht who invited him in for an interview the following day.[16] Knecht hired him and a year later Glazer quit law school to pursue a life in Hollywood. As law clerk for Warner Bros. Glazer delivered contracts to Hollywood's top executives and actors and started to have conversations about how television shows and movies were made. As he explained in his 2015 publication *A Curious Mind: The Secrete to a Bigger*

Life, his curiosity allowed him to be prepared for the opportunity that presented itself.[17] Over time, Glazer leveraged that one year law clerk position into a career as a producer, developing television projects. "It was while he was executive-producing TV pilots for Paramount Pictures in the early 1980s that Grazer first met Ron Howard, soon to become his friend and business partner. Their collaboration began in 1985 with the hit comedies *Night Shift* (1982) and *Splash*, and in 1986 the two founded Imagine Entertainment, which they continue to run together as chairmen."[18] While Grazer and Howard continue to collaborate in the entertainment industry, one relatively new and growing field of collaboration can be found in the power of crowds and their use of technology to support projects around the world.

The Power of Crowds

Successful people are now learning to leverage a new form of engagement with others due to recent technological advancements. Thanks to the advent of high-speed Internet connections, mobile devices, and online platforms, successful people have added crowdsourcing and crowdfunding as two new tools in their arsenal. Crowdsourcing is defined as the process of obtaining needed services, ideas, or content by soliciting contributions through the Internet. By definition, crowdsourcing combines the efforts of numerous self-identified volunteers or part-time workers, where each contributor, acting on their own initiative, adds a small contribution that combines with those of others to achieve a greater result. Crowdfunding is the practice of funding a project or venture by raising monetary contributions from a large number of people.

The crowdfunding model is based on three types of actors: the project initiator who proposes the idea and/or project to be funded; individuals or groups who support the idea; and a moderating organization (the "platform") that brings the parties together to launch the idea. Both crowdsourcing and crowdfunding have disrupted the ability to succeed at both the organizational and individual levels. Crowdsourcing uses the input of individuals external to an organization to resolve strategic problems or complete tasks once assigned internally to an explicit corporate individual or department. Widely dispersed contributors acquired through an open call for participation pinpoint data or offer opinions essential to achieving a specific objective for a designated problem. Open innovation for new products is also encouraged. Crowdsourcing participants encompass a population from everywhere, with all backgrounds; today's mobile functionality has made the potential assembly of contributors truly global in scope.

Crowdsourcing is the process of enlisting the help of a big crowd of people, usually on the Internet, whose collective knowledge, resources, and skills can help to come up with diverse and expert solutions to your problems. It is rapidly becoming a procedure of choice for generating innovative solutions issues for issues at the individual, social, and organizational levels. Examples of crowdsourcing include the following:

- *Anheuser-Busch*: While its *Budweiser* is easily America's best-selling beer, AB sought customer input to develop a brand more attuned to craft beer tastes. Development of *Black Crown*, a golden amber lager, combined a competition between company-brewmasters with consumer suggestions and tastings; this project had more than 25,000 consumer-collaborators.
- *Coca-Cola*: Its "Where Will Happiness Strike Next?" series of short films and TV commercials relies on the social media–input of Coke customers, contributing ideas about creating happiness. Coke also seeks crowdsourced online suggestions for marketing its products more effectively, once again tying social media to cocreation.
- *InnoCentive*: It is a Waltham, Massachusetts-based crowdsourcing company that accepts by commission research and development problems in engineering, computer science, math, chemistry, life sciences, physical sciences, and business. The company frames these as "challenge problems" for anyone to solve. It gives cash awards for the best solutions to solvers who meet the challenge criteria with The Rockefeller Foundation to add a nonprofit area designed to generate science and technology solutions to pressing problems in the developing world. Between 2006 and 2009, The Rockefeller Foundation posted 10 challenges on InnoCentive with an 80 percent success rate.

- *General Mills*: This major food-processing firm has created the *General Mills Worldwide Innovation Network* (G-WIN) to vigorously generate innovative concepts from crowdsourced partners in a variety of merchandise, commodity, or service categories. Included are products fitting the GenMil-brand concept, packaging of those products, and improvements to manufacturing, service or marketing processes to name just a few.
- *Nokia*: Like most crowdsourcing ventures, Nokia's Ideasproject defines itself as a global community devoted to open innovation. It focuses on consumer-derived collaboration across 210 nations to improve the viability of Nokia products in all markets.

In addition to crowdsourcing, crowdfunding has also ushered in a new form of collaboration. According to Massolution's *2015 Crowdfunding Industry Report*, global crowdfunding experienced accelerated growth in 2014, expanding by 167 percent to reach $16.2 billion raised, up from $6.1 billion in 2013. In 2015, the industry is set to more than double once again, on its way to raising $34.4 billion. The strong growth in 2014 was due in part to the rise of Asia as a major crowdfunding region. Asian crowdfunding volumes grew by 320 percent, to $3.4 billion raised. That puts the region slightly ahead of Europe ($3.26 billion) as the second biggest region by crowdfunding volume. North America continued to lead the world in crowdfunding volumes, growing by 145 percent and raising a total of $9.46 billion. Business and entrepreneurship remained as the most popular crowdfunding category, collecting $6.7 billion in 2014, which represents 41.3 percent of total crowdfunding volume. Social causes ($3.06 billion), films and performing arts ($1.97), real estate ($1.01 billion), and music and recording arts ($736 million) rounded out the top five categories.

Gofundme, kickstarter, and indiegogo are currently the top three crowdfunding sites. There are over 2,000 crowdsourcing sites available today.[19] The table below lists the top projects funded through GoFundMe.

Top projects funded through gofundme[20]

Project	Amount raised	Notes
Saving Eliza	$1,845,540 (as of 06/22/2015)	Saving Eliza is a campaign about Eliza O'Neill, a 5-year-old girl diagnosed with Sanfilippo syndrome. The campaign is funding urgent research to stop the terminal and rapidly degenerative disease in children. Saving Eliza today stands as the most ever raised on GoFundMe for a single campaign.
Bucks for Bauman	$809,310	This project was created for Jeff Bauman, after he lost both legs during the 2013 Boston Marathon bombings.
Celeste & Sydney Recovery Fund	$795,985	Both Celeste and Sydney Corcoran were victims of the 2013 Boston Marathon bombings. Sydney suffered severe injuries as a result of being hit with shrapnel, and Celeste lost both legs below her knees. This campaign page was created for their ongoing rehabilitation.
Hope for a Home	$410,011	After beating cancer twice, 22-year-old Melissa Smith was diagnosed with transverse myelitis, leaving her paralyzed from the waist down. Melissa's sister created this page to make Melissa's home handicap accessible. Her story was featured on The Chive, and the majority of the money raised for this project was donated in the first 24 hours from other Chive users.
Save Fisher More	$298,333	Faced with the closure of their school, the students of Fisher More College in Fort Worth, Texas, created this page to keep their doors open.
Christopher Lane Fund	$171,705	After Australian athlete, Christopher Lane, was shot and killed in Oklahoma, Marshall Veal created a fund so Christopher's family could return his body to Melbourne.

In addition to using the power of collaboration, leveraging the new tools of crowdsourcing and crowdfunding, successful people engage with others by intentionally placing themselves in open networks.

Open Networks

According to research published in the *Harvard Business Review* and elsewhere, what differentiates a leader from a manager is the ability to figure out where to go and to enlist the people and groups necessary to get there.[21] Recruiting stakeholders, lining up allies and sympathizers, diagnosing the political landscape, and brokering conversations among unconnected parties are all part of a leader's job. As they step up to the leadership transition, some managers accept their growing dependence on others and seek to transform it into mutual influence. Others dismiss such work as "political" and, as a result, undermine their ability to advance their goals.[22] Now more than ever, however, businesses are reaching beyond the boundaries of their organizations, tapping experts, customers, and, more broadly, "the crowd" to build new products, services, and other solutions.[23] In today's hyper-competitive global marketplace there is little time to discount the value of connecting with those outside the normal circle.

The old adage "it's now what you know, it's who you know" is true but there is a caveat. The "who you know" needs to be outside of the circles frequently traveled. Just being connected, or having a large number of LinkedIn contacts, fails to provide the necessary level of engagement often required to succeed. Research from network science shows that being the most connected person is not an effective way to build a network. Successful people intentionally work on engaging with those they have yet to connect with or those less connected. People with ties to the less-connected are more likely to hear about ideas that haven't gotten exposure elsewhere, and are able to piece together opportunities in ways that less effectively networked colleagues cannot.

In a research handout prepared as a basis for discussion in executive education for the University of Chicago, Booth School of Business, Professor Ronald S. Burt, discussed his findings on "Network Brokerage: How the Social Network Around You Creates Competitive Advantage for Innovation and Top-Line Growth." Most people spend their careers in closed networks; networks of people who already know each other. People often stay in the same industry, the same religion, and the same political party. In a closed network, it's easier to get things done because you've built up trust, and you know all the shorthand terms and unspoken rules. It's comfortable because the group converges on the same ways of seeing the world that confirm your own. People in open networks have unique challenges and opportunities. Because they're part of multiple groups, they have unique relationships, experiences, and knowledge that other people in their groups don't. This is challenging in that it can lead to feeling like an outsider as a result of being misunderstood and under-appreciated because few people understand why you think the way you do. It is also challenging because it requires assimilating different and conflicting perspectives into one worldview.[24]

According to the latest research, simply being in an open network instead of a closed one is the best predictor of career success.[25] Intentionally building an open network of engagement provides an individual with a variety of benefits that include the following:

- **A more accurate view of the world: an open network provides individuals** with the ability to pull information from diverse clusters so errors cancel themselves out. Research by Philip Tetlock shows that people with open networks are better forecasters than people with closed networks.
- **Ability to control the timing of information sharing.** While they may not be the first to hear information, they can be the first to introduce information to another cluster. As a result, they can leverage the first move advantage.
- **Ability to serve as a translator/connector between groups.** They can create value by serving as an intermediary and connecting two people (or organizations) who can help each other who wouldn't normally run into each other.
- **More breakthrough ideas.** Brian Uzzi, Professor of Leadership and Organizational Change at the Kellogg School of Management, performed a landmark study where he delved into the tens of millions of academic studies throughout history. He compared their results by the number of citations (links from other research papers) they received and the other

papers they referenced. A fascinating pattern emerged. The top performing studies had references that were 90 percent conventional and 10 percent atypical (i.e., pulling from other fields). This rule has held constant over time and across fields. People with open networks are more easily able to create atypical combinations.[26]

Conclusion

English actor and comedian John Cleese remarked in a 1991 interview that "creativity is not a talent; it is a way of operating."[27] In his 1950 work *The Art of Scientific Investigation* researcher W.I.B. Beveridge examined how scientists operated and discovered findings that pre-date Cleese's observation by decades but clearly support the premise that creativity is a way of operating. For Beveridge, one common theme he found evidence for time and again was "the eclecticism of influence necessary for true originality and the idea that creativity is combining and connecting things."[28] According to Beveridge, "Successful scientists have often been people with wide interests. Their originality may have derived from their diverse knowledge. Originality often consists in linking up ideas whose connection was not previously suspected."[29]

Decades ago, Beveridge understood the value of engaging with others outside the normal social networks one travels. Collaboration, leveraging crowds, and intentionally placing one's self in open network are three critical forms of engagement with others that successful people rely on to move forward. The way people collaborate, however, will continue to change due to the ongoing technological revolution. Successful people are constantly thinking about the possibilities of billions of people around the world connecting via social media, new media, and other forms of media. Successful people understand that younger generations will have jobs not yet developed using technology not yet invented to solve problems not yet identified. Engaging with others in the future will continue to challenge individuals who want to translate their dreams into reality. Successful people make engagement with others a priority. Do you?

Questions and resources for characteristic #2: Engage with others

Reading List

- Chris Gardner, *The Pursuit of Happyness: Start Where You Are*
- *Extreme Ownership: How US Navy SEALs Lead and Win*
- Keith Sawyer's *Group Genius: The Creative Power of Collaboration*
- Jeff Howe, *Crowdsourcing: Why the Power of the Crowd is Driving the Future of Business*
- James Surowiecki, *The Wisdom of Crowds*
- Clay Shirky, *Here Comes Everybody: The Power of Organizing without Organizations*
- Don Tapscott, *Wikinomics: How Mass Collaboration Changes Everything*
- Paul W. Mattessich, Marta Murray-Close, Barbara R. Monsey, *Collaboration: What makes it work, a review of research literature on factors influencing successful collaboration*

Questions

- When is the last time you collaborated with someone?
- Did you initiative your last collaboration or did someone else?
- Do you place a priority on engaging with others?
- Do you allow yourself to be open to receiving invitations of engagement from others?
- When is the last time you proactively sough to collaborate with someone?
- When is the last time you were asked to collaborate with someone?
- Have you engaged in crowdsourcing? If so, what has been your experience?
- Have you engaged in crowdfunding? If so, what has been your experience?
- Do you work or socialize in a closed network or an open network?
- Are you intentionally placing yourself in open networks? Why? Why not?
- Have you leveraged technology in any way to collaborate with others?

- What in your work improves the odds that you will discover the value of something you don't know?
- Have you completed The Wilder Collaboration Factors Inventory? If not, see the link below for more information.

Online Assessment

- The Wilder Collaboration Factors Inventory, a free online collaboration assessment is located at http://wilderresearch. org/tools/cfi/index.php: also included in *Collaboration: What makes it work, a review of research literature on factors influencing successful collaboration (2nd ed.).*

Progress is impossible without change, and those who cannot change their minds cannot change anything.

—George Bernard Shaw

Endnotes

1. A few of the many books on collaboration include: Michael Schrage, *Shared Minds: The New Technologies of Collaboration,* Random House, New York 1990, Danwa Markova and Angie McArthur, *Collaborative Intelligence: Thinking with People Who Think Differently*, Random House, New York, 2015 and Daniel Goleman and Richard Boyatzis, *HBR's 10 Must Reads on Collaboration*, Harvard Business Review, 2013

2. Michael Schrage, "Collaboration, from the Wright Brothers to Robots," *Harvard Business Review*, March 23, 2015.

3. David McCullough, *The Wright Brothers*, Simon & Schuster: New York, 2015.

4. Ibid.

5. Nick Glass and Tim Hume, "The 'hallelujah moment' behind the invention of the Post-it note," *CNN*, April 4, 2013.

6. Art Fry and Spencer silver, as told to Sarah Duguid, "First Person: 'We invented the Post-it Note,'" *Financial Times*, December 3, 2010.

7. Ibid.

8. A PDF of The Wilder Collaboration Factors Inventory can be found at www.wilder.org/Wilder-Research/Research-Services/Documents/Wilder%20Collaboration%20Factors%20Inventory.pdf.

9. Jimmy Wales, Wikipedia entry accessed December 2, 2015.

10. Jimmy Wales, "The birth of Wikipedia," TED talk, August 2006.

11. Wikipedia entry, Wikipedia, accessed December 20, 2015

12. Luke Malone, "The bike helmet that's invisible," *The Sydney Morning Herald*, November 15, 2013. Also see the introductory video at http://vimeo.com/43038579.

13. Michael Shermer, "As Luck Would Have It," *Scientific American*, March 26, 2006. Also visit Richard Wiseman's blog at www.richardwiseman.com/Luck.shtml.

14. Ibid.

15. Ibid.

16. Brian Grazer and Charles Fishman, *A Curious Mind: The Secret to a Bigger Life*, Simon & Schuster, New York, 2015.

17. Ibid.

18. Brian Grazer, IMDb biography, www.imdb.com/name/nm0004976/bio.

19. View the directory of crowdfunding links at www.crowdsourcing. org/directory.

20. https://en.wikipedia.org/wiki/GoFundMe.

21. Herminia Ibarra and Mark Lee Hunter, "How Leaders Create and Use Networks," *Harvard Business Review*, January 2007.

22. Ibid.

23. Brook Manville, "You Need a Community, Not a Network," *Harvard Business Review,* September 15, 2014.

24. Michael Simmons, "The No. 1 Predictor of Career Success According to Network Science," *Forbes*, January 15, 2015.

25. Ibid.

26. Michael Simmons, "The No. 1 Predictor of Career Success According to Network Science," *Forbes*, January 15, 2015.

27. Maria Popova, "John Cleese on the 5 Factors to Make Your Life More Creative," brainpickings blog, April 12, 2012.

28. Maria Popova, "The Art of Chance-Opportunism in Creativity and Scientific Discovery: A 1957 Guide, brainpickings blog, May 25, 2012.

29. Ibid.

CHAPTER 3

Commit to Lifelong Learning

Introduction

Dale Chihuly is an American artist, glass sculptor and entrepreneur. He specializes in blown glass and his works are considered highly specialized, unique and often classified as large-scale sculpture. Working with glass is considered a highly technical skill that demands precision, focus, and a commitment to life-long learning. Unfortunately, two terrible accidents would force Chihuly to change his career path. A 1976 traffic accident in England blinded his left eye and three years later he dislocated his right shoulder in a bodysurfing accident. These two events prohibited Chihuly from holding the pipe involved with glass blowing. Not to be deterred he hired others to do the work. Unable to create the glass art he taught others and learned how to become "more choreographer than dancer, more supervisor than participant, more director than actor."[1] Chihuly demonstrated what successful people so often do, the ability to commit to life-long learning.

In a small but impactful publication entitled *The Measure of Our Success: A Letter to My Children and Yours*, Marian Wright Edelman, American activist and founder of the Children's Defense Fund, wrote that one should never "stop learning and improving your mind or you are going to get left behind."[2] Futurist and best-selling author Alvin Toffler echoed similar thoughts when reflecting on how individuals can succeed in today's hypercompetitive and ever-changing global marketplace. Toffler concluded that "the illiterate of the 21st century will not be those who cannot read and write, but those who cannot learn, unlearn, and re-learn."[3] With disruptive technologies altering entire industries, causing drastic change in how people work, communicate, live, and just do about everything else, committing to lifelong learning will be a prerequisite to success. As one observer noted, "Keep learning, keep pushing yourself intellectually. With a great education and a mindset for growth, you will be able to live freely and chart your own course in changing times, and that will always be fulfilling."[4] *Making a commitment to lifelong learning requires one to engage in a growth mindset, understand the focusing illusion, and exhibit emotional intelligence.*

Practice the Growth Mindset

The Irish playwright George Bernard Shaw once observed, "People are always blaming their circumstances for what they are. I do not believe in circumstances. The people who get on in this world are the people who get up and look for the circumstances that they want, and if they can't find them, make them." While Shaw has a point, it might be more exact to say that "the people who get on in this world" have a growth mindset. In her 2006 publication *Mindset: The New Psychology of Success*, Carol Dweck, the Lewis and Virginia Eaton Professor of Psychology at Stanford University, concluded that people have either "fixed" or "growth" mindsets.[5] Those with a fixed mindset believe that "they are the way they are." This mindset believes that one's level of athleticism and mathematical capacities are fixed and have little room for improvement. Believing they are born with a certain amount of talent, fixed mindset individuals seldom challenge their abilities due to the possibility of failure. Fixed mindset individuals see improvement as a zero-sum game where there is a chance of failure. Those with a growth mindset, however, believe that they can improve by exercising their brain through hard work and practicing skills like athleticism. Growth mindset individuals have a desire to improve and view such development, even with its risk of failure, as a positive-sum game. This dedication to improvement drives growth mindset individuals forward despite great odds. How both mindsets approach challenges further illustrates the difference.

By definition, challenges are things that you decide to do. You decide to run a marathon, finish college, or get a new job. Such challenges are usually difficult and success is far from assured. Fixed mindset people need to maintain a positive self-image, so rather than risk failing, they will often avoid challenges and stick to what they do well. As a result, they seldom engage in situations where they feel a need to improve themselves. Challenges are frequently viewed negatively, instead of as an opportunity for personal growth. Growth mindset individuals, however, view failure in a far more positive light, see it as a chance to improve and ask themselves the question that Paul Arden challenged readers to answer: "How good do you want to be?" in his book *It's Not How Good You Are, It's How Good You Want to Be*. If you fail to understand the answer to that question, it may be difficult to embrace challenges you need to address to succeed in life. In the end, growth mindset people work hard at answering the question and embrace life's challenges along the way. Two people who practiced a growth mindset were entrepreneur Madame Walker and actor Jon Hamm.

Born Sarah Breedlove, Madame Walker moved in with her older sister and brother-in-law, Willie Powell after her parents died. To escape Powell's mistreatment, 14-year-old Sarah married Moses McWilliams and three years later gave birth to her daughter Lelia.[6] When Sarah was 20, her husband died, so she and her daughter moved to St. Louis where three of her brothers lived and worked in a barbershop. In 1906, she married Charles Joseph Walker, a newspaper advertising salesman. Because most Americans lacked indoor plumbing, central heating and electricity, Sarah, like most women, bathed and washed her hair infrequently and experienced hair loss and scalp disease.

To address this need, Sarah experimented with home remedies and products already on the market until she finally developed her own shampoo and an ointment that contained sulfur to make her scalp healthier for hair growth. While a fixed mindset person would have quit after the first few rounds of failure, Madame Walker figured out a way to sell her products throughout the country and then opened Lelia College to train other African-American women as hair culturists selling the Walker line of products. With a dedication to self-improvement throughout both her personal and professional life, Madame Walker eventually became the first self-made African-American female millionaire in the United States. She practiced the growth mindset. Jon Hamm is an American actor and director who asked himself, "How good do I want to be?" and then practiced a growth mindset to answer the question.

Both of Hamm's parents died before he was 21 years old. After graduating from the University of Missouri in 1993 with a Bachelor of Arts degree in English, Hamm returned to his high school to teach eighth-grade acting. With Paul Rudd as a friend and a desire to act for a living, Hamm moved out to Los Angeles with an automobile and $150 in 1995. His older appearance made it difficult to find employment, however, and after three years he was dropped by the William Morris agency. A fixed mindset individual would have viewed such a development as a failure. Instead, Hamm continued working as a waiter and set his 30th birthday as a deadline to succeed in Hollywood.

His belief was that "You either suck that up and find another agent, or you go home and say you gave it a shot, but that's the end of that. The last thing I wanted to be out here was one of those actors who are 45 years old, with a tenuous grasp of their own reality, and not really working much. So I gave myself five years. I said, 'If I can't get it going by the time I'm 30, I'm in the wrong place.' And as soon as I said that, it's like I started working right away." Eventually, he landed the role of the advertising executive Don Draper in the AMC drama series Mad Men, which premiered in July 2007. The Draper role earned him a Golden Globe Award for Best Actor in a Drama Series in 2008. Reflecting back upon his experiences, Hamm believes that "Losing both parents at a young age gave me a sense that you can't really control life—so you'd better live it while it's here. I stopped believing in a storybook existence a long time ago. All you can do is push in a direction and see what comes of it."[7] In addition to maintaining a growth mindset, successful people understand the focusing illusion.

Understand the Focusing Illusion

The focusing illusion is also known as the focusing effect and is a cognitive bias that occurs when people place too much importance on one aspect of an event, causing an error in accurately predicting the utility of a future outcome. In his 2011 book, *Thinking Fast and Slow*, the 2002 Nobel Prize recipient in Economics, Daniel Kahneman, discussed his concept of the focusing illusion and defined it as meaning "Nothing in life is as important as you think it is while you are thinking about it."[8]

To identify the focusing illusion you have to think hard. Since people "are not accustomed to thinking hard, they are often content to trust a plausible judgment that quickly comes to mind."[9] He applied the focusing illusion to education and wrote, "Education is an important determinant of income—one of the most important—but it is less important than most people think."[10] When the focusing illusion is applied to the issue of a successful career, salary is an important determinant of success—but it is less important than most people think. Other factors, such as having a flexible work schedule, engaging in meaningful work, and developing new professional skills, also play a critical role in having a successful career. Perhaps, nowhere is the focusing illusion more apparent than in the discussion between one's college major and future earnings income potential.

Evidence suggests little correlation between one's level of education or academic major and long-term income potential. "In a 2012 survey, 93 percent of employers agree that a candidate's demonstrated capacity to think critically, communicate clearly, and solve complex problems is more important than their undergraduate major."[11] "I think we are probably all focused a little too much on what is the undergraduate major and what is the hot major and what is the hot field . . . becoming a liberally educated and hardworking professional and getting some experience even if in the end you might end up changing fields is probably the better advice."[12] "It doesn't matter what you focus on, as long as you focus on it in a rigorous way."[13] Daniel Hamermesh of the University of Texas concluded that "Perceptions of the variations in economic success among graduates in different majors are exaggerated. Our results imply that given a student's ability, achievement and effort, his or her earnings do not vary all that greatly with the choice of undergraduate major."[14] While disparities do indeed exist in the beginning of one's career when certain majors are compared to others, "such financial disparities grow less pronounced over time as the 30 percent gap that separates academic and career-oriented majors at the start of their careers nearly vanish nine years later."[15]

Please understand that the evidence overwhelmingly demonstrates that "education is an important determinant of income but it is less important than most people think."[16] Focusing solely on education prevents the consideration of the myriad of other factors that determine income.

In other words, no one degree is necessarily better than another when moving up the corporate ladder or earning potential.[17] Such poor correlation between major and income can be attributed to many factors that affect individual earnings.[18] A few examples of the many factors that impact long-term income potential and career success include the following:

1. **Understand the impact of geography**: Where you live plays an important role in your ability to have a sustained career. For example, current research strongly suggests that looking for work in large urban areas can give workers a better chance to find a job that fits their skills. Additionally, in terms of salary and long-term career earnings, where you live often matters more than what you have on your résumé. Upon analyzing two decades of data from more than 200 cities, Rebecca Diamond, an assistant professor of economics at Stanford Graduate School of Business, found that college graduates are increasingly clustering in more expensive cities that offer more amenities such as restaurants and cultural attractions, better parks, less crime, and less pollution. To help recent college graduates identify key geographical locations, top 10 lists of cities to launch a career are now commonplace.[19]

2. **Market your value**: In my book *Marketing Your Value: 9 Steps to Navigate Your Career*, I explained that college students and even more experienced professionals need to work hard at helping employers understand their value. Doing so requires substantial work if you want to stand out among other job candidates. It is also important to understand that "being average just won't earn you what it used to. It can't when so many more employers have so much more access to so much more above average cheap foreign labor, cheap robotics, cheap software, cheap automation, and cheap genius."[20] You need to define yourself and what you are looking for in terms of employment. Give people reasons to pay attention to you. This is important to do in person as well as online. The only people who stand out are those who want to.

3. **Recognize the dynamics of compensation**: Focusing solely on your salary in and of itself demonstrates a severe lack of professional maturity. In his 1967 publication *The Motivation to Work*, Frederick

Herzberg identified two different categories of factors affecting the motivation to work: hygiene and motivation. Hygiene factors include extrinsic factors like technical supervision, interpersonal relations, physical working conditions, salary, company policies and administrative practices, benefits, and job security. In comparison, motivation factors include intrinsic factors such as achievement, recognition and status, responsibility, challenging work, and advancement in the organization. Herzberg's theory postulates that only motivation factors have the potential of increasing job satisfaction. The results indicate that the association between salary and job satisfaction is very weak. When employees are focused on external rewards, the effects of intrinsic motives on engagement are significantly diminished. This means that employees who are intrinsically motivated are three times more engaged than employees who are extrinsically motivated by money.

4. **Grow personally to develop professionally**: In today's challenging global economy, "individuals are under unprecedented pressure to develop their own abilities more highly than ever before, quote apart anything their employers may or may not do to develop them."[21] Personal discipline, growth, and a commitment to lifelong development are critical elements that factor into one's ability to achieve and sustain growth over a long career. In *The Start-up of You: Adapt to the Future, Invest in Yourself, and Transform Your Career*, authors Reid Hoffman (cofounder of LinkedIn) and Ben Casnocha realize that great people, like great organizations, are in a state of perpetual growth. "They're never finished and never fully developed." Each day presents an opportunity to learn more, do more, and grow more. This state of "permanent beta is a lifelong commitment to continuous personal growth" is a necessity for everyone regardless of what major you declared.

5. **Know that the reality is that people change jobs**: You may have a job after graduation but it will most likely not be your last. Layoffs, quitting, and a host of other reasons explain why people move from one job to another. In 2011, 48,242,000 people changed jobs in the United States. Of those who changed jobs, 20 million were from layoffs and discharges, 23 million workers quit, and 4 million were

classified as other separations.[22] With 131 million total workers, the 48 million people who changed jobs represented 36.7 percent of the total working population. Also, it is impossible to know what you want to do with the rest of your life at 22 when you have no idea what new jobs will exist in a decade or two. Today's graduates will have jobs not yet created using technology not yet invented to solve a problem not yet identified.

As professor Peter Cappelli of The Wharton School at the University of Pennsylvania observed, "it seems that what a person studies in college should relate to his or her planned career path, but it turns out that it's very hard to predict how those two things will interact with each other."[23] Successful people understand the focusing illusion as it relates to their undergraduate major and long-term income potential. In addition to practicing the growth mindset and understanding the focusing illusion, successful people also intentionally develop their emotional intelligence.

Develop Emotional Intelligence

In his widely recognized publication *Emotional Intelligence*, Rutgers University psychologist Daniel Goleman defines emotional intelligence (EI) as emotional management and the ability to identify, appropriately express, and manage our emotions. Over the last decade, there have been several studies illustrating the relationship between EI and career success. Ernest O'Boyle Jr. at Virginia Commonwealth University concluded that EI is the strongest predictor of job performance. The U.S. Air Force found that the most successful recruiters scored significantly higher on the EI competencies of empathy and self-awareness. A survey of 251 executives in six countries by Accenture identified three key indicators of EI that predicted future professional success: interpersonal competence, self-awareness, and social awareness.[24]

With growing evidence that EI is a strong indicator of career success, it behooves individuals to recognize its growing importance and commit to furthering their EI. Cognitive ability alone will not ensure career success. Successful people understand the need to combine sophisticated levels of cognitive and noncognitive skills with EI to successfully launch and navigate a career in today's hypercompetitive global economy. Since developing EI is important for personal, family, and business relationships, here are four of the many factors successful people often demonstrate:

1. *Self-awareness*: You maintain a realistic sense of self-confidence and understand your feelings. These two elements to self-awareness is the foundation upon which your EI can grow.
   a. *Realistic self-confidence*: You understand your own strengths and limitations; you operate from competence and know when to rely on someone else on the team.
   b. *Emotional insight*: You understand your feelings. Being aware of what makes you angry, for instance, can help you manage that anger.
   c. *Resolving Conflicts*: You maintain self-control and awareness to resolve conflicts peacefully and without emotion.
2. *Self-management*: Your ability to manage yourself through resilience and emotional balance allow you to keep moving toward short- and long-term goals simultaneously.
   a. *Resilience*: You stay calm under pressure and recover quickly from upsets. You don't brood or panic. In a crisis, people look to the leader for reassurance; if the leader is calm, they can be, too.
   b. *Emotional balance*: You keep any distressful feelings in check—instead of blowing up at people, you let them know what's wrong and what the solution is. You can successfully manage your emotions during times of stress.
   c. *Self-motivation*: You keep moving toward distant goals despite setbacks.
3. *Empathy*: Your understanding of other's perspectives, grounded in good listening skills, demonstrates your high degree of empathy.
   a. *Cognitive and emotional empathy*: Because you understand other perspectives, you can put things in ways colleagues comprehend. And you welcome their questions, just to be sure. Cognitive empathy, along with reading another person's feelings accurately, makes for effective communication.
   b. *Good listening*: You pay full attention to the other person and take time to understand what they are saying, without talking over them or hijacking the agenda.

c. *Perspective*: You understand and accept that the emotions of oth-ers are just as important as yours.

d. *Acceptance of criticism*: You leave emotion out of conversations regarding your performance and accept constructive criticism to improve your abilities.

4. *Relationship skills*: Your excellent communication skills allow you to develop strong team work among a diverse group of people who feel relaxed around you.

a. *Compelling communication*: You put your points in persuasive, clear ways so that people are motivated as well as clear about expectations.

b. *Team playing*: People feel relaxed working with you. One sign: They laugh easily around you.

c. *Acceptance of Others*: You get along with and work well with oth-ers, even if you do not like them. You do not allow you emotions to have a negative impact on others.

Conclusion

Successful people commit to lifelong learning, which requires maintain-ing a growth mindset, understanding the focusing illusion, and exhib-iting emotional intelligence. *Fortune* Magazine Senior Editor at Large Geoff Colvin links the need for lifelong learning to professional and personal success in *Humans Are Underrated: What High Achievers Know That Brilliant Machines Never Will*. To build a competitive advantage, organizations need to focus on the social interaction skills of relation-ship building, cultural sensitivity, empathy, and self-awareness. At the individual level, Colvin argues that career success depends upon one's ability to differentiate from competitors. To accomplish this, he suggests individuals become more wholly human by recognizing their feelings as well as those of others because how people feel profoundly influences how they perform.[25] To be more fully human in the emerging world of work, Colvin emphasizes the value and application of the humanities over special-ized fields of study like science, technology, engineering, or math. The skills nurtured by studying the humanities "are precisely those that the economy will increasingly value."[26] Successful people understand that lifelong learn-ing demands that they remain open to learning throughout their life to continuously update their ability to be more fully human and engaging.

Questions and resources for characteristic #3: Commit to lifelong learning

Readings

- Carol Dweck, *Mindset: The New Psychology of Success*
- Paul Arden, *It's Not How Good You Are, It's How Good You Want To Be*
- Daniel Kahneman, *Thinking, Fast and Slow*
- Daniel Goldman, *Emotional Intelligence: Why It Can Matter More Than IQ*
- Richard H. Thaler, *Nudge: Improving Decisions About Health, Wealth and Happiness*

Questions

- Madame Walker demonstrated a growth mindset by teaching herself how to move forward despite many obstacles. Have you?
- Hamm asked himself, "How good do I want to be?" and then kept pushing until he answered that question. Have you?
- How often do you ask yourself how good you want to be?
- Have you helped someone achieve the level of how good they wanted to be?
- How often do you examine whether your mindset is fixed or growing?
- Have you suffered from the focusing illusion?
- Why do you think people experience the focusing illusion?
- What can you do to understand when you are experiencing the focusing illusion?
- Have you helped someone understand that they are experiencing the focusing illusion?

Growth Mindset Quiz

Directions: This quiz tests your awareness of the differences between growth and fixed mindsets. For each of the following statements, write down whether it belongs to a fixed or growth mindset. Answers are on the following page. For example: "Intelligence is something people are born with that can't be change." Does that statement belong to someone who a growth or fixed mindset?

1. Intelligence is something people are born with that can't be changed.
2. No matter how intelligent you are, you can always be more intelligent.
3. You can always substantially change how intelligent you are.
4. You are a certain kind of person, and there is not much that can be done to really change that.
5. You can always change basic things about the kind of person you are.
6. Musical talent can be learned by anyone.
7. Only a few people will be truly good at sports you have to be "born with it."
8. Math is much easier to learn if you are male or maybe come from a culture who values math.
9. The harder you work at something, the better you will beat it.
10. No matter what kind of person you are, you can always change substantially.
11. Trying new things is stressful for me and I avoid it.
12. Some people are good and kind and some are not; it's not often that people change.
13. I appreciate when people, parents, coaches, teachers give me feedback about my performance.
14. I often get angry when I get negative feedback about my performance.
15. All human beings are capable of learning.
16. You can learn new things, but you can't really change how intelligent you are.
17. You can do things differently, but the important parts of who you are can't really be changed.
18. Human beings are basically good, but sometimes make terrible decisions.
19. An important reason why I do my school work is that I like to learn new things.
20. Truly smart people do not need to try hard.

Questions

- What three or five statements above do you agree with? Why is that?
- Can you demonstrate examples from your life for two or more of the statements?
- Have you seen others exemplify one or more of these statements?

Answers to Growth Mindset Quiz

1. Intelligence is something people are born with that can't be changed. FIXED
2. No matter how intelligent you are, you can always be more intelligent. GROWTH
3. You can always substantially change how intelligent you are. GROWTH
4. You are a certain kind of person, and there is not much that can be done to really change that. FIXED
5. You can always change basic things about the kind of person you are. GROWTH
6. Musical talent can be learned by anyone. GROWTH
7. Only a few people will be truly good at sports you have to be "born with it." FIXED
8. Math is much easier to learn if you are male or maybe come from a culture who values math. FIXED
9. The harder you work at something, the better you will beat it. GROWTH
10. No matter what kind of person you are, you can always change substantially. GROWTH
11. Trying new things is stressful for me and I avoid it. FIXED
12. Some people are good and kind and some are not; it's not often that people change. FIXED
13. I appreciate when people, parents, coaches, teachers give me feedback about my performance. GROWTH
14. I often get angry when I get negative feedback about my performance. FIXED

15. All human beings are capable of learning. GROWTH
16. You can learn new things, but you can't really change how intelligent you are. FIXED
17. You can do things differently, but the important parts of who you are can't really be changed. FIXED
18. Human beings are basically good, but sometimes make terrible decisions. GROWTH
19. An important reason why I do my school work is that I like to learn new things. GROWTH
20. Truly smart people do not need to try hard. FIXED

The illiterate of the 21st century will not be those who cannot read and write, but those who cannot learn, unlearn, and relearn.
—Alvin Toffler

Endnotes

1. Dale Chihuly, Wikipedia, accessed December 21, 2015.

2. Marian Wright Edelman, *The Measure of Our Success: A Letter to My Children and Yours*, William Morrow Paperbacks, New York, 1993.

3. Guofang Wan and Dianne M. Gut, Editors, *Bringing Schools into the 21st Century*, Springer Dordrrecht Heidelberg, London, 2011.

4. Daniel R. Porterfield, "The Future for Today's College Graduates Is Uncertain. . . . But They Can Handle It," *Forbes*, May 5, 2014.

5. For more growth mindset information found in this chapter visit Dweck's website: http://mindsetonline.com/abouttheauthor/.

6. A few of the many resources on Madame Walker include *Wikipedia*, http://en.wikipedia.org/wiki/Madam_C._J._Walker; *Biography*, www.biography.com/people/madam-cj-walker-9522174#synopsis; and *PBS*, www.pbs.org/wnet/african-americans-many-rivers-to-cross/history/100-amazing-facts/madam-walker-the-first-black-american-woman-to-be-a-self-made-millionaire/.

7. Two of the many resources on Jon Hamm include: *Wikipedia*, http://en.wikipedia.org/wiki/Jon_Hamm; and *Vanity Fair*, www.vanityfair.com/online/oscars/2009/08/mad-men-qa-jon-hamm.

8. Daniel Kahneman, *Thinking, Fast and Slow*, Farrar, Straus and Giroux, New York, 2013.

9. Daniel Gardner, *The Science of Fear*, Penguin, New York, 2008.

10. David Brooks, "Tools for Thinking," *The New York Times,* March 28, 2011.

11. Lynn O'Shaugnessy, "What Employers Want in College Grads," *CBS Money Watch*, April 16, 2013.

12. Leslie Eastman, "Business Leaders Say Communication Skills, Critical Thinking More Important than Major," *College Insurrection*, April 17, 2013.

13. Jeffrey J. Selingo, "Does the College Major Matter? Not Really," *The New York Times*, April 29, 2013.

14. Zac Bissonnette, "Your College Major May Not Be As Important As You Think," *The New York Times*, November 3, 2010.

15. Dan Berrett, "Debate Continues over Merits of Liberal Arts Education," *Pocono Record*, July 1, 2010.

16. David Brooks, "Tools for Thinking," *The New York Times,* March 28, 2011.

17. Louis Lavelle, "Accidental Moguls: College Majors of Top CEOs," *Bloomberg BusinessWeek*, May 17, 2010.

18. Elka Maria Torpey, "The Class of 1993: Earnings and Occupations by College Major, 1 and 10 Years after Graduation," *Occupational Outlook Quarterly*, Summer 2008.

19. "Top 10 Best Cities for Post Grads," April 3, 2015, www.rent.com.

20. Thomas L. Friedman, "Average Is Over," *The New York Times*, January 24, 2012.

21. Geoff Colvin, *Talent Is Overrated: What Really Separates World-Class Performers from Everybody Else*, New York, Penguin Books, 2008.

22. "Quick Stat: 48 Million People (37% of the Workforce) Changed Jobs in 2011," *Net Perspectives*, March 20, 2012.

23. Bourree Lam, "The Danger of Picking a Major Based on Where the Jobs Are," *The Atlantic*, June 12, 2015.

24. Ray Williams, "The Biggest Predictor of Career Success? Not Skills or Education-but Emotional Intelligence," *Financial Post*, January 1, 2014.

25. Tony Schwartz, "Humanity as a Competitive Advantage," *The New York Times*, September 18, 2015.

26. Geoff Colvin, "Liberal Arts Majors: Rejoice! Technologists Are Learning They Need More than STEM to Create Appealing Products," *Salon*, August 8, 2015.

CHAPTER 4

Increase Your Self-Awareness

Introduction

Hazel Rose Markus' 1986 paper "Possible Selves" redefined how psychologists think of the relationship between self and culture. In that paper she and coauthor Paula Nurius developed the concept of possible selves: the ideal self we would like to become, we could become, and we are afraid of becoming.[1] "A person's identity involves more than the thoughts, feelings and behaviors of the current self; it also includes reflections of what a person was like in the past and hopes and fears about what a person may become in the future."[2] Each individual has a repertoire of possible selves that serve as the "cognitive manifestation of enduring goals, aspirations, motives, fears, and threats [which] provide the essential link between the self-concept and motivation."[3] To suggest that there is a single self to which one "can be true" or an authentic self that one can know is to deny the rich network of potential that surrounds individuals and that is important in identifying and descriptive of them.[4] Possible selves contribute to the fluidity or malleability of the self because they are differentially activated by the social situation and determine the nature of the working self-concept. At the same time, the individual's hopes and fears, goals and threats, and the cognitive structures that carry them are defining features of the self-concept; these features provide some of the most compelling evidence of continuity of identity across time. Successful people understand that they have an active role in developing who they would like to become and work hard at doing so. Such a process involves a substantial amount of experiencing, reflecting, and meaning-making throughout one's entire life. Successful people understand the value of maintaining a high level of self-awareness. They ask themselves important questions and keep doing so throughout their life. One of the most important questions successful people ask themselves is "Why am I doing what I am doing?" The story of Sir Christopher Michael Wren serves as an excellent example.

After the Great Fire of London in 1666, Sir Christopher Michael Wren, one of the most highly acclaimed English architects in history, had the responsibility for rebuilding 52 churches, including his masterpiece, St. Paul's Cathedral. The cathedral was built in a relative short time span: its first stone was laid on June 21, 1675, and the building was completed in 1711. Legend has it that Wren would often visit the construction site. During one of his visits, Wren came across three stonecutters. Each was busy cutting a block of stone. Interested to find out what they were working on, he asked the first stonecutter what he was doing. "I am cutting a stone!" Still no wiser, Wren turned to the second stonecutter and asked him what he was doing. "I am cutting this block of stone to make sure that it is square, and its dimensions are uniform, so that it will fit exactly in its place in a wall." A bit closer to finding out what the stonecutters were working on but still unclear, Wren turned to the third stonecutter. He seemed to be the happiest of the three and when asked what he was doing, replied: "I am helping to build a great cathedral." This stone mason clearly understood *why* he was doing *what* he was doing. Both Wren and the third stone mason understood that they were part of something greater than themselves. They were experiencing the richness of life. This richness allows one to develop their self, which is a never-ending process throughout life. Jocko Willink and Chris Gardner are two modern day examples of successful people who maintain a high level of self-awareness.

Retired US Navy SEAL commander Jocko Willink sets three alarms each morning: one electric, one battery-powered, and one windup. In *Extreme Ownership: How US Navy SEALs Lead and Win*, coauthored with Leif Babin, Willink says that "discipline starts every day when the first alarm clock goes off in the morning."[5] He sets three alarm clocks because "there is no excuse for not getting out of bed, especially with all that rests on that *decisive moment*."[6] He is, however, not the only successful person that has a high level of self-awareness with an understanding of how to effectively manage time. On the cover of his book *The Pursuit of*

Happyness: Start Where You Are, entrepreneur Chris Gardner has a watch on each wrist. It's not until page 160 that he explains why.[7] One day, Gardner, a stockbroker calling on new account leads, was late to a prospective client. He failed to close the account but took to heart what his prospective client told him, "Son if I can't expect you to be on time, I can't expect you to make timely decisions with my money."[8] From that point onward, Gardner started to wear a watch on each wrist so as never to be late again. The stories of Willink and Gardner may seem extreme, but they illustrate two excellent examples of the second characteristic successful people often demonstrate: they work hard at maintaining a high-level of self-awareness. *Successful people increase their self-awareness by determining their self, marketing their value, and meditating.*

Determine Your Self

Successful people learn how to engage in self-determination. Self-determination theory (SDT) is an approach to human motivation and personality that articulates enhanced performance, persistence, and creativity, arguably three critical skills everyone needs to succeed, best fostered by an individual developing a sense of autonomy, competence, and relatedness.[9] These three traits, autonomy, competence, and relatedness, are characteristics often found in successful people. Co-developed by two University of Rochester psychology professors, Edward L. Deci and Richard M. Ryan, SDT "focuses on the social-contextual conditions that facilitate versus forestall the natural processes of self-motivation and healthy psychological development."[10] According to Deci and Ryan, "Excessive control, non-optimal challenges, and lack of connectedness disrupt the inherent actualizing and organizational tendencies endowed by nature, and thus such factors result not only in the lack of initiative and responsibility but also in distress and psychopathology."[11] Unfortunately, many parents today are demonstrating excessive control over their child's life and are prohibiting their child's self-determination. An epidemic of hyper-involvement known as helicopter parenting has emerged during the last three decades.[12] Helicopter parents often micromanage every decision, dictate schedules, and control relationships for their children.[13]

This invasive parenting prohibits students from creating the sense of autonomy, competence, and connectedness required to determine their own sense of self. This level of involvement actually sends the wrong message to children.[14] For example, for those parents who contact the college admissions officer, professor, or coach with the intention of trying to resolve a situation on behalf of their child, they are sending an unintentional message that their child is incompetent. Such an approach is counterproductive to fostering a child's ability to determine their self. Harvard psychiatrist Dr. Dan Kindlon concluded that parents who protect children from discomfort or failure actually insulate them from experiences that can facilitate growth and resilience.[15] Children need to practice self-determination by experiencing autonomy, self-reliance, and connecting with others. In this context, one can indeed practice the characteristics of self-determination. By interfering in a child's life, however, the parent is undermining a child's ability to problem-solve, communicate, and persevere through a difficult situation. These are three critical skills every professional needs to develop throughout their entire career.

Stunting their growth early on places children at a disadvantage throughout high school and even after they graduate college. Throughout their entire development children of helicopter parents often have little, if any, exposure to autonomy, competence, and relatedness, "When adult children don't get to practice problem-solving skills, they can't solve these problems in the future."[16] Well-meaning and misguided parents inadvertently foster a sense of "existential impotence whereby their child lacks the self-awareness, is unable to make choices, and has difficulty coping with setbacks."[17] Staying connected via technology has only exacerbated the problem. By constantly texting, Facebook messaging, or Skyping for daily check-ins, parents further their child's codependency on them. Such hovering is counterproductive to a child's maturity. As one mother said, "When you hover, you take away that sense of self-esteem."[18] Self-determination demands that a child resolve problems, work through challenging situations, and have difficult conversations with others on their own. The journey to self-discovery is lifelong and best made with the child learning how to navigate their own lives. The helicopter parenting epidemic is so serious that one expert proclaimed: "Parents who don't encourage their sons and daughters to be independent are guilty of psychological abuse."[19]

Fostering self-determination in a child is hard work. The more a parent interferes, disrupts or prohibits their child's self-determination, the more challenging it is for the child to have a genuine sense of self. Supporting a child's ability to self-determine involves nurturing their skills and abilities, understanding their thoughts and feelings, and enabling them to dream and aspire. "When parents decide for their children rather than help them to decide for themselves, children become dependent, not independent, compliant rather than adventurous."[20] Becoming dependent and compliant on a parent makes it extremely challenging for a twenty-something to then deal with one of life's inevitable experiences: failure.

Part of self-determination is experiencing failure, disappointment, and discomfort and learning how to work through each situation. Unfortunately, helicopter or snowplowing parents shield their children from even the slightest degree of discomfort. Failure is a distant shore that children of intrusive parents seldom see. Children are sometimes home-schooled to prevent them from being exposed to people, ideas, and material the parents deem inappropriate. Prohibiting children from people or ideas you deem uncomfortable for your child to process and then expecting them to mature into well-adjusted, autonomous adults able to connect with others is simply unrealistic.[21] As one mother said, "We need to let our kids chart their own course and make their own mistakes."[22] Competence is one of the three foundational elements of self-determination, but children need to learn that they can't be good at everything. To learn lessons of failure, disappointment, or discomfort, children need to experience those things as early as elementary school. Such lessons should be reinforced since high school students, college students, and young professionals need to experience disequilibrium but at greater levels. Doing so can prepare equip them with the skills necessary to deal with life's issues throughout adulthood. The experience of psychological and cognitive disequilibrium produces feelings of internal "dissonance" that manifests itself as uncertainty, and sometimes as conflict and even threat.[23] "But it is the experience of such dissonance that opens up the possibility for learning and growth because it nudges students into confronting and considering new ways of understanding, thinking, and acting that help to unsettle the old and integrate it with the new."[24]

UCLA psychiatrist Paul Bohn believes many parents will do anything to avoid having their child experience even mild discomfort, anxiety, or disappointment.[25] Shielding a child from psychological and cognitive disequilibrium, failure, or discomfort provides a tremendous disservice; "with the result that when, as adults, they experience the normal frustrations of life, they think something must be terribly wrong."[26] "It is essential for students' learning and growth in college to have challenging stimuli and experiences of positive restlessness because these provide the creative disequilibrium and intellectual foment that drive personal exploration and development."[27]

In their 2012 book *The Start-up of You: Adapt to the Future, Invest in Yourself, and Transform Your Career,* authors Reid Hoffman (cofounder of LinkedIn) and Ben Casnocha realize that great people, like great organizations, are in a state of perpetual growth. "They're never finished and never fully developed. Each day presents an opportunity to learn more, do more, and grow more. This state of permanent beta is a lifelong commitment to continuous personal growth."[28] As today's dynamic global marketplace continues to present organizations with new challenges to address, problems to solve, and questions to answer, executives and human resource managers are going to need people dedicated to personal growth.

In one study of human resource directors conducted in the United Kingdom, 91 percent of respondents think that by 2018, prospective employees will be recruited on their ability to deal with change and uncertainty. Over half of the respondents said one of their key attribute for future business success is finding individuals who are able to deal with unanticipated problems.[29] In today's volatile and uncertain global economy, if you lack personal development, it may be difficult to move forward because protectionist measures from governments, companies, and unions are disappearing. Professional development is directly linked to personal growth. If you want to grow as a professional you will need to grow as a person. *Your* specific contribution will define *your* specific benefits much more. "Just showing up will not cut it."[30]

Stressing the relationship between personal growth and professional success, Robert S. Kaplan, Emeritus Professor of Leadership Development at the Harvard Business School, observed that "fulfillment doesn't come from clearing hurdles others set for you; it comes from clearing those you set for yourself."[31] Throughout his career, Kaplan realized that ambitious professionals spend a substantial amount of time thinking about strategies that will help them achieve greater levels of success. By striving for a more impressive job title, higher compensation, or increased responsibility, ambitious professionals often allow their definition of success to be influenced by family, friends, and colleagues. Despite their achievements and high level of success, Kaplan found that many ambitious professionals lacked a true sense of professional satisfaction and fulfillment. Kaplan wrote that he met a large number of "impressive executives who expressed deep frustration with their careers. They looked back and felt that they should have achieved more or even wished that they had chosen a different career altogether."[32]

Market Your Value

Successful people work hard at finding new ways to market their value to a complete stranger. "The real challenge for recent college graduates is deciding how to apply their fundamental skills to the line of work you choose for yourself. But take note: Employers aren't going to figure it out for you. You have to figure it out for yourself."[33] The key is that you have to differentiate yourself from other candidates. "Being average just won't earn you what it used to. It can't when so many more employers have so much more access to so much more above average cheap foreign labor, cheap robotics, cheap software, cheap automation, and cheap genius. Therefore, everyone needs to find their unique value contribution that makes them stand out in their field of employment."[34] "Define yourself and your purpose. Broadcast your strengths. Give people a reason to pay attention to you. It's your choice to do something worth talking about or not. The only people who stand out are those who want to."[35] Successful people intentionally position themselves in the minds of others.

By definition, positioning is a marketing term used to describe the process by which marketers create an image or identity in the minds of their target audience for a specific product, service, or organization. A professional competing in today's challenging economy needs to position his or her genuine self in the minds of prospective employers in a clear, concise, and compelling fashion. Remember, each individual has the responsibility to learn how to advocate for their own interests, skills, and goals. Effectively communicating one's value is a pre-requisite to the achievement of professional development. Doing so requires hard work, determination, and a substantial amount of thought. Professionals at every level have an expectation that their degree or experience will have immediate and obvious value in the job market. Please understand that this is far from reality. One's degree, experience, and current position are important but what will have a greater impact on an ability to navigate a career is the ability to market one's value. Although it remains taxing to find employment, the real challenge is deciding how to position one's value in the marketplace so potential employers can clearly understand it. During the last 10 years, the emergence of social media has mandated that people think differently about how they position themselves to people they do not even know.

The advent of social network sites has changed the environment for job seekers in general and college graduates specifically. Every professional needs to constantly monitor their behavior both off-line but especially on-line. The issue of online personal brand management is so important and pervasive that Google's Eric Schmidt said, "Parents will have to have the 'online privacy' talk with their children before 'the sex talk'" and "It might be when they're eight years old, you'll be saying 'don't put that online! It'll come back to bite you!' and then have to explain why."[36] Two recent trends highlight the imperative that is online privacy and personal brand management: firms are using social network sites to review potential candidates who have submitted credentials for a specific position and to also identify potential talent that can help them fill a vacancy.

With statistics varying, one thing is certain, more employers from almost any industry are now checking social media sites for information about a person who has applied for a job. Employers and human resource officials routinely "admit that they have made hiring decisions based on what they saw on those social networking sites, largely to the candidate's detriment. For example, HR representatives have eliminated job applicants from the screening process where their social media sites have revealed inappropriate photographs, alcohol or drug use, unsatisfactory communication skills, prejudice, dishonesty about their qualifications, derogatory comments about their previous employers or coworkers, disclosure of a former employer's proprietary information, and the like."[37]

While screening a candidate via an online search might seem harsh for some, the flip side is that "more than half of human resource professionals are tapping into social networking websites to look for in potential job candidates, a significant increase from 2008."[38] When reviewing someone's credential, approximately 56 percent of organizations reported scanning LinkedIn, Facebook, Twitter, and other professional networking sites for recruitment purposes in 2012, compared with 34 percent who used the same social networks to find new employees in 2008. "Employers are increasingly using social networking sites to engage passive job seekers—those who aren't really actively seeking new jobs but might change for the right opportunity," said Mark J. Schmit, PhD, SPHR, director of research at SHRM. "These sites can be valuable tools for organizations to find prospective employees with the specific skill sets and experience that they might not necessarily find through more traditional recruiting methods."[39]

One final note here on positioning yourself involves an important lesson of intention and interpretation. In a 2010 Baccalaureate address titled "We Are What We Choose," Jeff Bezos, the CEO of Amazon, recalled a trip he took with his grandparents when he was young. During a road trip, his grandmother started to smoke in the car. Bezos, a self-proclaimed precocious 10-year-old, laboriously calculated the damage to her health that his grandmother was doing by smoking. His conclusion was that, at two minutes per puff, she was taking nine years off her life. When he proudly told her of his finding, she burst into tears. His grandfather stopped the car, pulled alongside the road and said to Bezos: "One day you'll understand that it's harder to be kind than clever."[40] In his speech, Bezos went on to distinguish between gifts and choices. "Cleverness," he said, "is a gift. Kindness is a choice. Gifts are easy—they're given, after all. Choices can be hard." He then challenged the graduating students to think carefully about their future range of choices: "Will you be clever at the expense of others, or will you be kind?"[41] To garner this level of self-awareness, many successful people engage in meditation or activities that increase their mindfulness.

Meditate

To determine their self or market their value, successful individuals will often increase their self-awareness through some form of meditation or mindfulness. Stanford psychologist and best-selling author Kelly McGonigal wrote "My favorite definition of the mindful path is the one the reveals itself as you walk down it. You cannot find the path until you step on to it."[42] While walking on the path is critical to success, so too is reflecting upon life's experiences. Successful people learn from their mistakes and also reflect upon those that others made. One of the most common forms of reflection is meditation, also referred to as mindfulness. Recent research on the link between meditation and its link to the brain has substantially increased our understanding on the benefits of mindfulness. Although the systematic study of meditation is still in its infancy, the American Mindfulness Research Association (AMRA) has a scientific database of over 3,200 academic publications on mindfulness from a contemplative psychology and practice perspective.

According to the AMRA, the number of research papers on meditation or mindfulness went from three in 1980 to 535 in 2014.[43] The research has provided evidence for meditation-induced improvements in psychological and physiological well-being, as well as benefitting higher-order cognitive functions and altering brain activity.[44] "Meditation research, particularly in the last 10 years or so, has shown to be very promising because it points to an ability of the brain to change and optimize in a way we didn't know previously was possible."[45] For example, research has found that meditators who had practiced five years or more had "significantly larger volumes" of gray matter in the hippocampus, an area crucial to memory and learning. For example, several studies have shown that mindfulness reduces rumination. In another study, researchers asked 20 novice meditators to participate in a 10-day intensive mindfulness meditation retreat. After the retreat, the meditation group had significantly higher self-reported mindfulness and a decreased negative affect compared with a control group. They also experienced fewer depressive symptoms and less rumination. In addition, the meditators had significantly better working memory capacity and were better able to sustain attention during a performance task compared with the control group.

Regular meditation, in other words, might help one grow more brain.[46] It is important to note that this research is in its infancy and "future longitudinal analyses are necessary to establish the presence and direction of a causal link between meditation practice and brain anatomy."[47]

Neuroscientist Richard J. Davidson's groundbreaking research on Tibetan Buddhist monks at the University of Wisconsin-Madison has found that years of meditative practice can dramatically increase neuroplasticity—the brain's ability to use new experiences or environments to create structural changes. For example, it can help reorganizing itself by creating new neural connections. "The findings from studies in this unusual sample suggest that, over the course of meditating for tens of thousands of hours, the long-term practitioners had actually altered the structure and function of their brains."[48]

Since 2008, Zoran Josipovic, a research scientist and adjunct professor at New York University, has been peering into the brains of monks while they meditate in an attempt to understand how their brains reorganize themselves during the exercise. Dr. Josipovic, who also moonlights as a Buddhist monk, is hoping to find how some meditators achieve a state of "nonduality" or "oneness" with the world, a unifying consciousness between a person and their environment. "One thing that meditation does for those who practice it a lot is that it cultivates attentional skills," Dr. Josipovic says, adding that those harnessed skills can help lead to a more tranquil and happier way of being.[49] This tranquil way of living can also help individuals cope with the death of a loved one or their own demise. Eugene O'Kelly's diagnosis with an inoperable brain cancer serves as one example.

When he was diagnosed with an inoperable brain cancer, Eugene O'Kelly, the then 53-year-old American chief executive of the accounting firm KPMG, wrote *Chasing Daylight: How My Forthcoming Death Transformed My Life*. O'Kelly died on September 10, 2005, but in the months leading up to his passing, he discovered the world around him and connected with nature, time, and loved ones as never before. In short, death increased his self-awareness on an entirely new level. During his final months, he would sometimes invite a friend or acquaintance to take a stroll in the park. Such a stroll, according to O'Kelly "was sometimes not only the final time we would take such a leisurely walk together, but also the first time." This level of self-awareness is often found in individuals experiencing terror management theory.

For over four decades, the field of social psychology has provided a theory of human motivation toward achievement known as terror management theory (TMT). Anthropologist Ernest Becker's 1973 publication *The Denial of Death* helped launch the field of TMT. Since the publication of his book, researchers have conducted over 200 experiments investigating TMT.[50] Becker received a Pulitzer Prize for his nonfiction work two months after his death from cancer at the age of 49. TMT proposes a basic psychological conflict that results from having a desire to live but realizing that death is inevitable. An award winning documentary *Flight from Death* also examines Becker and his TMT research.[51] To clarify, terror in this case not being associated with the term terrorism, typically defined as the use of violence and intimidation in the pursuit of political aims, but rather emotional and psychological reaction to mortality awareness. TMT involves mortality salience, also referred to as death cognition that is defined as the point in a person's life when they become aware that death is inevitable.

TMT theory argues most human action is taken to ignore or avoid the inevitability of death and suggests that "death cognition does not lead to death anxiety because people respond to thoughts of death by turning to social and cultural structures that provide a sense of psychological security."[52] The terror of absolute annihilation creates a profound subconscious, and perhaps conscious anxiety in people that they spend their lives attempting to make sense of it. According to Becker: "The idea of death, the fear of it, haunts the human animal like nothing else; it is a mainspring of human activity—activity designed largely to avoid the fatality of death, to overcome it by denying in some way that it is the final destiny for man." As humans pursue activities designed to avoid the fatality of death, some interesting findings have recently been discovered.

New studies conducted by researchers at the University of Missouri concluded that maintaining an awareness of life's end may increase one's positive outlook. Contemplating death doesn't necessarily lead to morose despondency, fear, aggression, or other negative behaviors, as previous research has suggested. The paper "When Death is Good for Life: Considering the Positive Trajectories of Terror Management" was published on April 5, 2012, in *Personality and Social Psychology Review*, a journal of the Society for Personality and Social Psychology. This research found that thoughts of mortality can lead to decreased militaristic attitudes, better health decisions as well as increased altruism and helpfulness. Additionally, an awareness of mortality can motivate people to enhance their physical health and prioritize growth-oriented goals; live up to positive standards and beliefs; build supportive relationships and encourage the development of peaceful, charitable communities; and foster open-minded and growth-oriented behaviors. While death awareness can, at times, generate negative outcomes, it can also function to move people along more positive trajectories and contribute to the good life.[53] As one of the lead researchers observed "Once we started developing this study we were surprised how much research showed positive outcomes from awareness of mortality,"[54] In his 2005 Stanford University commencement speech, Steve Jobs reflected on the value of thinking about death and echoed similar sentiment when he said "Remembering that I'll be dead soon is the most important tool I've ever encountered to help me make the big choices in life. Death is the destination we all share and your time is limited so don't waste it living someone else's life."

Conclusion

In an oft-quoted 1990 speech, John W. Gardner, former Secretary of Health, Education and Welfare under President Lyndon Johnson, echoed similar sentiment and suggested that "When you get to the top you stand up and look around and chances are you feel a little empty. Maybe more than a little empty. You wonder whether you climbed the wrong mountain." Gardner observed that life is neither a mountain to summit, a riddle to answer, or a game to win. Instead, "Life is an endless unfolding, and if we wish it to be, an endless process of self-discovery, an endless and unpredictable dialogue" between our own capacities for learning, sensing, wondering, understanding, loving, and aspiring and the life situations in which we find ourselves.[55]

Frenchman Philippe Petit lived a life centered around an endless process of self-discovery. In 1974, Petit took a calculated risk, which took years of planning, and walked across a tightrope between the Twin Towers of the World Trade Center in New York City. Knowing with one false step he could plummet 1,350 feet to the ground, Philippe walked back and forth eight times, totaling appropriately 45 minutes. Petit walked across the wire a week before his 25th birthday. He had been dreaming of making this walk since he had read about plans to construct the towers in a magazine when he was 17 years of age.[56] The 2009 film *Man on Wire* told Petit's story and won the Academy Award for best documentary. According to Petit "life should be lived on the edge of life. You have to exercise rebellion: to refuse to tape yourself to rules, to refuse your own success, to refuse to repeat yourself, to see every day, every year, every idea as a true challenge—and then you are going to live your life on a tightrope."

Questions and resources for characteristic #4: Increase self-awareness

Readings

- Geoff Colvin, *Humans Are Underrated: What High Achievers Know That Brilliant Machines Never Will*, 2015
- Michael Edmondson, *Major in Happiness: Debunking the College Major Fallacies*
- Kennon M. Sheldon, *Self-Determination Theory in the Clinic: Motivating Physical and Mental Health*, 2013
- Reid Hoffman and Ben Casnocha, *The Start-up of You: Adapt to the Future, Invest in Yourself, and Transform Your Career*
- Charles Duhigg, *The Power of Habit: Why We Do What We Do in Life and Business*
- Stephen R. Covey, *The 7 Habits of Highly Effective People: Powerful Lessons in Personal Change*

Questions

- Have you relied solely on your college major, grade point average or name of the institution to get you where you are in your career?
- What role have soft skills played in your development and success?
- How has your job or industry changed with the adoption and adaptation of computers or robotics?
- Have you relied solely on your expertise in one area to succeed?
- If you are a parent, how often do you support your child's self-determination?
- If you are a parent, how often do you allow your child to experience failure, disappointment, or discomfort?
- Are you clearing hurdles others set for you or those you have set for yourself?
- What have you done lately to grow personally?
- Can you provide an example of how personal growth is directly linked to professional development?
- How have others contributed to your definition of success?
- What do you need to do to take your personal development to the next level?
- Have you spent any time meditating?
- Have you thought about your legacy long after you have died?

Life belongs to the living, and he who lives must be prepared for changes.
—Johann Wolfgang von Goethe

Endnotes

1. Hazel Rose Markus and Paula Nurius, "How Many 'Selves' Do We Have?" *Being Human*, February 25, 2014.

2. Curtis Dunkel and Jennifer Kerpelman, editors, *Possible Selves: Theory, Research and Applications*, New York, Nova Science Publishers, Inc., 2006.

3. Hazel Rose Markus and Paula Nurius, "How Many 'Selves' Do We Have?" *Being Human*, February 25, 2014.

4. Ibid.

5. Richard Feloni, "Why this retired Navy SEAL commander has 3 alarm clocks and wakes up at 4:30 a.m.," *Business Insider*, October 25, 2015.

6. Ibid.

7. Chriis Gardner, *The Pursuit of Happyness,* Amistad, New York, 2006.

8. Ibid.

9. Self-determination Theory website: www.selfdeterminationtheory.org/theory/ (accessed August 6, 2015).

10. Richard M. Ryan and Edward L. Deci, "Self-Determination Theory and the Facilitation of Intrinsic Motivation, Social Development, and Well-Being," *American Psychologist*, Vol. 55, 2000, pp. 68–78.

11. Ibid.

12. Hara Estroff Marano, "Helicopter Parenting-It's Worse than You Think," *Psychology Today*, January 31, 2014.

13. Julie Lythcott-Haims, "Kids of Helicopter Parents Are Sputtering Out," *Slate*, July 5, 2015.

14. Kari Gude, "College Students and Their Helicopter Parents: a Recipe for Stress," *Huffington Post*, January 8, 2014.

15. Steve Baskin, "The Gift of Failure," *Psychology Today*, December 31, 2011.

16. Bonnie Rochman, "Hover No More: Helicopter Parents May Breed Depression and Incompetence in Their Children," *Time*, February 22, 2013.

17. Julie Scelfo, "Suicide on Campus and the Pressure of Perfection," *The New York Times*, July 27, 2015.

18. Amy Joyce, "How Helicopter Parents Are Ruining College Students," *Washington Post*, September 2, 2014.

19. Phillip Hodson, "My Message to the Parents Who Can't Let Their Children Go: Grow up," *The Guardian*, August 5, 2012.

20. Joseph D. Putti, *Searching for Inspiration?* Seems Awkward, Ignores the Rules, but Brilliant: Meet the Maverick Job Candidate," *TIME Magazine,*, 2013.

21. Kelly Wallace, "Longing for the Carefree Parenting Style of Yesterday?" *CNN News*, August 25, 2014.

22. Ibid.

23. Jon Dalton and Pamela Crosby, "Challenging College Students to Learn in Campus Cultures of Comfort, Convenience and Complacency," *Journal of College and Character*, Vol. 9, 2008, pp. 1–5.

24. Ibid.

25. Kari Kubiszyn Kampakis, "10 Common Mistakes Parents Today Make," *Huffington Post*, March 3, 2014.

26. Ibid.

27. Jon Dalton and Pamela Crosby, "Challenging College Students to Learn in Campus Cultures of Comfort, Convenience and Complacency," *Journal of College and Character*, Vol. 9, 2008, pp. 1–5.

28. For more information please visit *The Start Up of You* website: www.thestartupofyou.com/.

29. "The Flux Report: Building a Resilient Workforce in the Face of Flux," published by Right Management and Manpower Group, May 28, 2015.

30. Thomas L. Friedman, "It's a 401(k) World," *The New York Times*, April 30, 2013.

31. Richard S. Kaplan, "Reaching Your Potential," *Harvard Business Review*, July-August 2008.

32. Ibid.

33. Michele Menegay Marion, "Liberal Arts Is Slang for Job Skills," *Ask the Headhunter*, no date.

34. Thomas L. Friedman, "Average Is over," *The New York Times*, January 24, 2012.

35. John Morgan, *Brand against the Machine: How to Build your Brand, Cut through the Marketing Noise, and Stand out from the Competition,* Hoboken, NJ, John Wiley & Sons, Inc., 2011.

36. Dorotea Szkolar, "Facebook Hookup Apps: Privacy Disaster Waiting to Happen?" *Information Space,* March 25, 2013.

37. "Hiring Decision in the Age of Social Media," *The Greater Lansing Business Monthly,* no date.

38. Catherine Skrzypinski, "SHRM Poll: Social Networking Websites Popular as Employer Recruiting Tool, SHRM press released dated April 18, 2011.

39. Ibid.

40. "Amazon founder and CEO Jeff Bezos delivers graduation speech at Princeton University," YouTube video, 18:52, posted by Princeton Academics, June 11, 2010, www.youtube.com/watch?v=vBmavNoChZc.

41. Ibid.

42. Kelly McGonigal –True Willpower: How to Create Change through Self-Acceptance, Desire, and the Present Moment, podcast located on Emerging Women, 2013.

43. Visit https://goamra.org/resources/ for more information about the substantial growth in mindfulness research.

44. Eileen Luders, et al., "The Underlying Anatomical Correlates of Long-term Meditation: Larger Hippocampal and Frontal Volumes of Gray Matter," *Neuroimage,* Vol. 45, 2009, pp. 672–678.

45. Matt Danzico, "Brains of Buddhist Monks Scanned in Meditation Study," *BBC News,* April 24, 2011.

46. Zoe Schlanger, "The Neuroscience of Meditation, and the Virtues of Shutting Up," *Newsweek,* August 14, 2015.

47. Eileen Luders, et al., "The Underlying Anatomical Correlates of Long-term Meditation: Larger Hippocampal and Frontal Volumes of Gray Matter," *Neuroimage,* Vol. 45, 2009, pp. 672–678.

48. Richard J. Davidson, "Buddha's Brain: Neuroplasticity and Meditation," *IIEEE Signal Process Magazine,* January 2008.

49. Matt Danzico, "Brains of Buddhist Monks Scanned in Meditation Study," *BBC News,* April 24, 2011.

50. Brian L. Burke, et al., "Two Decades of Terror Management Theory: A Meta-Analysis of Mortality Salience Research," *Personality and Social Psychology Review*, Vol. 14, 2010, pp. 155–195.

51. The official website of this documentary is http://transcendentalmedia .com/new/films/now-playing/flight-from-death-the-quest-for-immortality/.

52. Clay Routledge, et al., "Mortality Salience Increases Death Anxiety for Individuals Low in Personal Need for Structure," *Motivation and Emotion*, Vol. 37, 2013, pp. 303–307.

53. Kenneth E. Vail III, et al., "When Death Is Good for Life: Considering the Positive Trajectories of Terror Management," Personality and Social Psychology Review, Vol. 16, 2012, pp. 303–329.

54. "The Bright Side of Death: Awareness of Mortality Can Result in Positive Behaviors, Say MIU Researchers," April 30, 2012.

55. John Gardner, "Personal Renewal" Delivered to McKinsey & Company, Phoenix, AZ, November 10, 1990.

56. Anthony Haden-Guest, "Philippe Petit's Moment of Concern Walking the WTC Tightrope," *The Daily Beast*, August 8, 2014.

CHAPTER 5

Remain Open
to the Possibilities

Introduction

The fifth characteristic that successful people demonstrate is remaining open to what is possible. Successful people understand that life is uncertain. "Uncertainty reveals limitation and limitation signals vulnerability; it exposes our limitation of knowledge and power, and it suggests that there may be potentials within us and possibilities around us."[1] Canadian psychoanalyst and organizational consultant Elliott Jaques coined the term "midlife crisis," in a 1965 paper.[2] Jaques wrote that during this period, individuals come face-to-face with their limitations, their restricted possibilities, and their mortality. In his own midlife and beyond, however, Jaques remained opened to the possibilities of what life had to offer and wrote 12 books in the 38 years between the publication of his paper that coined the term "midlife crisis," and his death in 2003 at age 86.[3] He also married Kathryn Cason and they founded a consulting company devoted to the dissemination of their ideas. Like Jaques, Dennis Farina left himself open to the possibilities of what life has to offer late in his career as well.

Dennis Farina left himself open to what is possible and enjoy a successful acting career founded upon serendipity. Before becoming an actor, Farina served three years in the US Army and then 18 years in the Chicago Police Department's burglary division, from 1967 to 1985.[4] He had been working as a detective when a mutual friend introduced him to the director Michael Mann, who was making his first feature film in 1981, "Thief." Mr. Farina was initially a consultant for the movie before being given a small role as a crime boss's enforcer. For several years afterward,

Mr. Farina juggled his police job with local theater roles and appearances in movies and television shows. He was often cast by Mr. Mann, including in several episodes of his hit show "Miami Vice."[5] Farina quit police work after Mr. Mann cast him in 1986 in the NBC series "Crime Story." He would go on to spend four decades in film and television with a two season stint in Law & Order as Detective Joe Fontana. Farina died in July 2013 and left behind a life filled with happiness, success, and opportunity due to serendipity. *By remaining open to what is possible, successful people think differently, experience disequilibrium, and place themselves in situations encouraging serendipity.*

Think Differently

Successful people understand that translating dreams into reality often involves the need to think differently. Life in the 21st century certainly challenges individuals to think differently about everything. We need to implement the process of thinking differently in our lives so that we become adaptable to the changes ahead. Amid today's ongoing disruptive developments, it is important to remind ourselves that "the truth about change is that we tend to overestimate its speed while underestimating its reach."[6] In order for individuals to succeed today, they "need a fresh set of insights, not a fresh set of instructions."[7] But thinking differently, and moving away from the usual way of doing things, approach to life and work is a formidable challenge since "people often refuse to relinquish their deep-seated beliefs even when presented with overwhelming evidence to contradict those beliefs."[8] As author Paul Arden wrote in his 2006 book *Whatever You Think, Think The Opposite*, people are trapped not because they make the wrong decisions, it's because they make the right ones. According to Arden, "We try to make sensible decisions based on the facts in front of us. The problem with making sensible decision is that so is everyone else."[9] As the current research indicates, both genetics and environment impact one's ability to think differently.

Harvard psychologist Shelley H. Carson explains that creativity is an activity open to everyone both at home and at work. Scientists, investors, artists, writers, and musicians are just a few of the many occupations that benefit from creativity. Teachers, engineers, and health-care professionals can all benefit from developing their creativity. Unfortunately, many adults limit their creative thinking. Carson's book *Your Creative Brain: Seven Steps to Maximize Imagination, Productivity, and Innovation in Your Life* found that 60 to 80 percent of adults find the task of thinking different uncomfortable and some even find it exhausting. Connecting the unconnected through associational thinking exhausts adults who have lost the creative skills once practiced throughout childhood. Unfortunately, the process of maturing from childhood to adulthood involves growing up in an environment that punishes anyone who thinks differently at home and at school. As Sir Ken Robinson noted in his 2006 TED talk "Do Schools Kill Creativity?" "People grow out of creativity; they get educated out of it." Education demands conformity and often runs counter to creativity that requires an individual to pursue a novel idea. Thinking differently requires someone to leave the "usual way of doing things" while risking failure, ridicule, and nonconformity. That exposure is very anxiety provoking for many people. In addition to the research on the anxiety related to thinking differently, there is also substantial new work in the field of neuroscience.

Neuroscience research during the last few years suggests that the right brain/left brain distinction fails to provide a comprehensive picture of how creativity is implemented in the brain. The belief that the left brain is realistic, analytical, practical, organized, and logical, while the right brain is creative, passionate, sensual, tasteful, colorful, vivid, and poetic is becoming less clear as more research is conducted. In short, the latest research suggests that no one side of the brain has a monopoly on creativity. "The entire creative process, from preparation to incubation to illumination to verification, consists of many interacting cognitive processes (both conscious and unconscious) and emotions."[10] Many different brain regions work together during the creativity process. Recent evidence suggests that "cognition results from the dynamic interactions of distributed brain areas operating in large-scale networks."[11] For those individuals who claim they are too right-brained to be creative, this new research challenges them to think differently about how they think. Using the right-brained approach to life is no longer an excuse. As creative people will tell you, neither is the fear of failure.

Highly creative people who think differently have figured out that failure is a learning experience and, as such, is a necessary and expected part of future success. So, while roughly one-third of anyone's innovation capacity comes from their genetic endowment, two-thirds of it is still driven by the environment. As Jeff Dyer and Hal Gregersen concluded, from their study of over 5,000 entrepreneurs and executives, almost anyone who consistently makes the effort to think different can do so. Individuals labeled as innovators of new businesses, products, and processes spend almost 50 percent more time trying to think different compared to non-innovators.[12] Two examples of individuals who thought differently and changed their respective worlds were high jumper Dick Fosbury and skier Émile Allais.

In the 19th-century, track and field athletes jumped over a horizontal bar for an event called the high jump. Athletes jumped over the bar using a straight-on approach or a scissoring of the legs technique as the jumper landed in sawdust landing pits. With advancements in the landing pads, jumpers started to implement the Western roll technique where the inner leg is used for the take-off while the outer leg is thrust up to lead the body sideways over the bar.[13] While athletes worked on improving their performance, Portland, OR, native Dick Fosbury eventually discovered a new technique during the 1960s that would revolutionize the event. Fosbury started jumping over bars in the fifth grade using the scissor kick technique and cleared 3 feet 10 inches.

"In high school, despite the dire warnings of every coach who watched him, he invented the 'Fosbury Flop' and reached 6 feet 7 inches. At the 1968 Mexico City Olympics, in front of 80,000 spectators, the 21 year old Fosbury cleared a record breaking 7 feet 41/4 inches."[14] After applying the Western roll technique for the early part of his career, Fosbury took advantage of the raised softer landing areas and leveraged such developments to think differently. During his running approach, he directed himself over the bar head and shoulders first, sliding over on his back and landing in a fashion that would likely have broken his neck in the old, sawdust landing pits. During Fosbury's early days of practicing his new technique at the University of Oregon, people said that his approach was unnecessary. The usual way of jumping over the bar was good enough. His approach went against the Best Practices of high jumping. Luckily,

Fosbury ignored those early critics and went on to establish a new way of thinking and jumping. Allais also ignored critics with his revolutionary approach to skiing.

Émile Allais was a daring champion French skier who helped shape his sport by developing and popularizing a new style of skiing in the 1930s with skis parallel to each other rather than angled inward in a V shape. The French Skiing Federation adopted that as its official style. Skiers all over the world, like high jumpers with the Fosbury Flop, started to use the parallel method of skiing. Simply by changing the position of his legs and skis, Allais helped promote a more smooth, efficient, and fun form of skiing.[15] Jean-Claude Killy, the French skier who dominated the sport in the late 1960s, credited Allais for teaching him to take risks and hailed Allais as "the father of modern skiing." Allais often challenged the status quo and did a somersault in an event and landed on his skis without losing time. *The New York Times* once described him as "a congenital candidate for the suicide club" and marveled at how he often seemed out of control before miraculously recovering. He impressed competitors so much that a German skier once called Allais "the greatest all-around skier the world has ever known."[16] Sometimes thinking differently also involves experiencing a sense of disequilibrium.

Experience Disequilibrium

Psychological and cognitive disequilibrium, an unsettling stimulus or experience that disrupts one's previously established belief structure, is a trait often found in the backstories of successful people. Disequilibrium can be produced by almost any stimulus that agitates one's current way of understanding and being. According to Nevitt Sanford, the experience of psychological and cognitive disequilibrium produces feelings of internal dissonance that manifests itself as uncertainty, and sometimes as conflict and even threat. "But it is the experience of such dissonance that opens up the possibility for learning and growth because it nudges individuals into confronting and considering new ways of understanding, thinking, and acting that help to unsettle the old and integrate it with the new."[17] This integration of the new with the old requires intention coupled with an increase in self-awareness. Experiencing disequilibrium requires one to take ownership of their learning and then proactively leverage the integration of the new with the old in order to grow.

This integration of the old with the new is the offspring of two different life situations: inspiration or desperation. Those who find themselves in desperate times might be forced to glean learning from disequilibrium. Having a loved one die suddenly, getting laid off from a long-term employment position, or not being able to find a fulfilling job for an extended period of time are just three examples of desperate times that create disequilibrium. Individuals who are thrust into these situations could directly contribute to their personal growth by reflecting and thinking about the value of disequilibrium for their own development. Others aim for inspiration and proactively take responsibility for their self-improvement. These individuals place themselves in learning environments and seek out disequilibrium to get comfortable in uncomfortable situations. Doing so challenges them to grow in new and exciting ways. Best-selling author Jim Rohn used to tell the story that his mentor, Earl Shoaff, once said to him, "If you want to be wealthy and happy, learn to work harder on yourself than you do on your job."[18] Shoaff's statement woke Rohn up and he continuously worked hard at his personal growth describing it as "the most challenging assignment of all that lasted a lifetime."

Seth Godin's 2012 publication *The Icarus Deception: How High Will You Fly?* echoes similar sentiment and wrote, "It's not about whether we have what it takes; it's about whether we choose to pursue it. The astonishing news is that for the first time in recorded history it matters not so much where you are born or what your DNA says about you—the connection economy is waiting for you to step forward, with only the resistance to hold you back."[19] But remember, the path you will travel when launching your career will take years and consist of "big moments of panic, insecurity, and fear. That's not because you are awful, and your life is awful."[20] Those are just normal feelings. "The good news is that these moments of realization, panic, and their aftermath will slowly teach you the perspective to define your own idea of what 'made it' is all about. For some, it's having kids, for others, no kids. Some hunger for the city, others dream of living on a farm, or the suburbs. When you feel yourself stressing about these things, relax. There is always another day. Don't worry about screwing up, you'll figure it out as you go along. That's how every person who's really 'made it' has done it."[21] One person who "really made it" is author Paulo Coelho.

Best-selling Brazilian author Paulo Coelho had many reasons to quit in his quest to be a writer. By relying on his commitment to personal growth, Coelho overcame a variety of issues throughout his life to become an award-winning author. Because he went against his parent's wishes who wanted him to be a lawyer, they sent him to an asylum where he received electroshock therapy. Coelho escaped three times between 16 and 20 years of age, and eventually appeased his parents and went to law school, but dropped out to become a hippy traveling through South America, North Africa, Mexico, and Europe.

During the late 1960s and early 1970s, he wrote lyrics for Raul Seixas, the Brazilian rock star and other artists. In 1974, Coelho was arrested for "subversive" activities by the ruling militia (bundled into a car, taken to a secret headquarters, and tortured with electric shock to his genitals). Looking for some normalcy, he went to work for Polygram record company. He eventually met his first wife, moved to London in 1977, but Coelho was unhappy and wanted to write, so he went back to Brazil and they divorced. He married twice more before settling down with an old friend, Christina Oiticica. "She is my fourth wife, and last," he said.

In 1982, he published his first book, *Hell Archives* but it failed to make an impact. In 1986, at 39 years of age, Coelho walked the 500 mile Road of Santiago de Compostela in northwestern Spain—the turning point in his life. The following year he wrote *The Alchemist,* an allegorical novel that tells the story of a young Andalusian shepherd named Santiago in his journey to Egypt, after having a recurring dream of finding treasure there. The first edition of *The Alchemist* sold only 900 copies and the publishing house decided not to reprint. With a lifelong commitment to personal growth, Paulo refused to quit and worked hard to translate his dream of being a writer into reality and found another publishing house. *The Alchemist* went on to sell more copies than any other book in Brazilian literary history. As Coelho wrote in *The Alchemist*, "To realize one's destiny is a person's only obligation." Eventually, Coelho would go on to publish 30 books and sold more than 150 million books in over 150 countries. His works have been translated into 80 languages and he is the all-time best-selling Portuguese language author. While Coelho remained open to the possible by thinking differently and working through many experiences of disequilibrium, successful people also place themselves in situations encouraging serendipity.

Remain Open to Serendipity

Serendipity is defined as the occurrence and development of events by chance in a happy or beneficial way. There are plenty of examples that illustrate how successful people learned to harness serendipity as a rigorous business practice.[22] To further investigate the impact of serendipity on success, researchers continue to assess the role of chance events in personal and professional development.[23] Researchers explain that one never has to decide what he or she will "be" in the future since despite setting goals at various times in one's career, these goals are always subject to change as one grows and learns and as the world changes. Furthermore, unplanned events will inevitably have unexpected impacts upon career plans. Researchers do, however, say that serendipity can be used to one's advantage if individuals develop skills to recognize, create and use these chance occurrences as they think about their careers. Critical attributes for taking advantage of serendipitous events are curiosity, persistence, flexibility, optimism, and risk-taking.[24]

Deborah G. Betsworth and Jo-Ida C. Hansen summarized their research on serendipity and career development in "The Categorization of Serendipitous Career Development Events," published in *Journal of Career Assessment*. In their research sample, 237 older adults completed a brief questionnaire that asked if their careers were influenced by serendipitous events. The results indicated that 63 percent of the men and 57 percent of the women felt that their careers were influenced by serendipitous events. Participants described 11 different categories of chance events (see Table 5.1).

There was no matchmaking service that brought together Lennon and McCartney, Jobs and Wozniak, or Ben and Jerry. Each of these people put themselves in motion—they escaped their isolated environments or routines long enough to bump into others. Circumstance brought these personalities together, but to achieve success they had to connect, see something in each other, and ultimately take the initiative in pursuing the partnership.[26] The popular Tom Cruise movie *Jerry McGuire* is based

Table 5.1 Categories of Chance Events[25]

Type of Chance Event	Description
Professional or personal contacts	Relationships with employers, friends, professors, advisors, or colleagues that lead to conversations, invitations, collaborations, or other formal or informal events.
Unexpected advancement	The resignation, firing, or death of a colleague and the subsequent selection or promotion into the vacated position.
Right place/time	Being open and prepared for the unexpected phone call or in-person conversation.
Influences of marriage and family	Impact of career choices of partners or health situation of family members.
Encouragement of others	Significant others, advisors, or mentors who encourage the pursuit of new fields.
Influence of previous work	Past volunteer or work experiences provide numerous opportunities to increase skills and interactions with others.
Military experiences	Military service influences career paths.
Temporary position becomes permanent	When a short-term assignment evolves into a long-term opportunity.
Obstacles in original career path	Obstacles (e.g., lack of jobs, financial strain, and unexpected illness) hindered career path.
Influence of historical events	Financial crisis, global weather events or other external factors beyond one's control.
Unintended exposure to field	An unexpected encounter with a field of interest not previously considered.

on the life of a high-powered professional sports agent, Leigh Steinberg. During the early 1970s, Steinberg was a student at the University of California at Berkeley, working his way through law school as a dormitory counselor and serving as student body president. Steinberg planned to pursue either a job opportunity with the County District Attorney's Office or opportunities in the field of environmental law. As luck would have it, the freshman football team moved into his dormitory. He befriended several of the student athletes, including one named Steve Bartkowski, who went on to become an outstanding professional football player. During his final year at the university, Bartkowski was selected as the first draft pick of the Atlanta Falcons. Bartkowski asked Steinberg to represent him in contract negotiations with the Falcons, and the rest is history because

Steinberg has gone on to represent many professional athletes and other celebrities during the last 20 years.[27]

Luis Echegoyen has held influential positions at major universities and the National Science Foundation, published extensively, and won national and international recognition for his work. But in a career that spans nearly 40 years, there has been one surprisingly consistent theme: serendipity. When Echegoyen spoke to a small group of 30 scientists and at a Summer Leadership Institute of the Society for the Advancement of Chicanos and Native Americans in Science in Washington, D.C., it was plain that he did not see serendipity as something light and whimsical. And he clearly wasn't talking about blind luck. Instead, he was talking about how scientists can structure their careers—and their lives—so that good but unplanned opportunities are more likely to emerge. "Serendipity is not strange," he said. "It's the norm. It's like mutations—it's happening all the time. . . . Of course you can't go through life thinking, 'Maybe something good will happen tomorrow.' You should have some kind of a plan. "[But] be aware of the limits of planning—I can't stress that enough. The more you connect, the more people you know, and the more diverse their backgrounds are, the better chance you have of something you did not anticipate happening."[28]

He was born in Cuba, where his father was a famous comedian; at the age of 9, his family bought round-trip tickets to Puerto Rico, but they never returned home. "I was 9 years old—I had no control over what was going on," he recalled. "This was completely serendipitous. . . .This is what life deals to you. This is what you have to live. But then you make it the best you can." As he grew up, he wanted to be a chemist—that was the plan. He got his Ph.D. at the University of Puerto Rico, and took a postdoctoral position. He hadn't decided whether to pursue a career in research and scholarship or in industry. "But it happened that Union Carbide was interviewing on campus," he said. "They knocked on my door and said, 'Are you interested in a job at Union Carbide?' When they told me the salary, I said, 'Sounds interesting.'" Within a couple of years, he had an invitation to join the faculty at UPR. That set a pattern that would assert itself repeatedly as the years went by: Opportunities that he had not sought and did not expect emerged, often arriving through people he had met or worked with along the way. He followed them to Miami, South Carolina, Washington, D.C., and Texas, with sabbaticals in France and Switzerland. [29]

Conclusion

By remaining open to what is possible, successful people think differently, experience disequilibrium, and place themselves in situations encouraging serendipity; all of which require a period of reflection and meaning-making for the individual. Thinking differently, disequilibrium, and serendipity challenge an individual to make meaning from new experiences and knowledge. This meaning-making allows an individual to achieve a new level of equilibrium and certainty about how the world operates. Research suggests that "the process of disequilibrium takes on a sequence of levels in which equilibrium must be established at lower levels before the individuals can attempt to make meaning of disequilibrium at a higher level."[30] Successful people understand this, or grow to realize this process, and gradually build the capacity to take on greater complexity in both thought and action over time. Another way of thinking about this is that successful people understand the benefit of getting out of their comfort zone. "Stepping outside one's comfort zone is an important, and almost universal, factor in personal growth. Reaching new heights involves the risk of attempting something we might not succeed at."[31] When evaluating the impact of people going out of their comfort zone, researchers have found that learning to adapt to a little anxiety can help people achieve to focus their efforts and perform at their peak in order to reach new levels of achievement. Stephen Josephson, a psychologist in New York City who has treated athletes, actors, and musicians noted that "coaches and sports psychologists have always known that they do not want their athlete to be relaxed right before an event as they need some 'juice' to go fast."[32] As Alina Tugend wrote in a *New York Times* editorial "being slightly uncomfortable, whether or not by choice, can push us to achieve goals we never thought we could." Recognizing that individuals don't need to challenge themselves all the time, Tugend concluded that although it is good to step out of our comfort zone, it is also good to go back in when necessary.[33]

Questions and resources for characteristic #5: Remain open to possibilities

Readings

- Paul Arden, *Whatever You Think, Think the Opposite*
- Shelley H. Carson, *Your Creative Brain, Seven Steps to Maximize Imagination, Productivity and Innovation in Your Life*
- Seth Godin, *The Icarus Deception: How High Will You Fly?*
- Simon Sinek, *Start with Why: How Great Leaders Inspire Everyone to Take Action*
- Simon Sinek, *Leaders Eat Last: Why Some Teams Pull Together and Others Don't*

Questions

- Do you proactively seek to think differently?
- Do you seek input from others to help you think differently?
- Have you helped others think differently?
- When is the last time thinking differently helped you succeed?
- Why do you think people hesitate to think differently?
- When is the last time you experienced psychological or cognitive disequilibrium?
- Have you intentionally placed yourself in situations where you would experience disequilibrium?
- Do you intentionally spend time thinking about your experiences of disequilibrium?
- Have you helped others process their experiences with disequilibrium?

Life is an endless unfolding, and if we wish it to be, an endless process of self-discovery, an endless and unpredictable dialogue between our potentialities and the life situations in which we find ourselves

—John Gardner

Endnotes

1. Robert Pryor and Jim Bright, *The Chaos Theory of Careers: A New Perspective on Working in the Twenty-First Century,* Routledge Press, New York, 2011.

2. Carolo Strenger and Arie Ruttenberg, "The Existential Necessity of Midlife Change,, *Harvard Business Review,* February 2008.

3. Ibid.

4. William Yardley, "Dennis Farina, Detective in Life and TV, Dies at 69," *The New York Times,* July 23, 2013.

5. Ibid.

6. Jeff Selingo, *College Unbound: The Future of Higher Education and What It Means for Students*, Amazon Publishing, Las Vegas, NV 2013. "Selingo, editor at large for *The Chronicle for Higher Education* and senior fellow at Education Sector, knows a thing or two about the need to think differently and argues that America's higher education system is broken. In the wake of the 2008 recession, colleges can no longer sell a degree at any price as the ticket to success in life. Brand-name universities like Harvard, Yale, Cornell, and Stanford will always find students and families willing to pay the sticker price because of their institution's global prestige, influential alumni networks, and considerable endowments. But the campuses that the vast majority of Americans attend, where some students go into tens of thousands of dollars in debt for degrees with little payoff, will need to adapt fast to the changing job market and new technological breakthroughs."

7. Youngme Moon, *Different: Escaping the Competitive Heard*, Crown Business, New York, 2011.

8. Brian Klapper, "Free Yourself from Conventional Thinking," *Harvard Business Review Blog*, May 6, 2013.

9. Paul Arden, *Whatever You Think, Think the Opposite*, Portfolio, New York, 2006.

10. Scott Barry Kaufman, "The Real Neuroscience of Creativity," *Scientific American*, August 19, 2013.

11. Ibid.

12. Jeff Dyer and Hal Gregersen, "Learn How to Think Different (ly)," *Harvard Business Review*, September 27, 2011.

13. Visit http://en.wikipedia.org/wiki/High_jump for more information on the history of the high jump.

14. Joseph Durso, "Fearless Fosbury Flops to Glory," *The New York Times,* October 20, 1968.

15. Douglas Martin, "Emile Allais, Haid as the Father of Modern Skiing, Dies at 100," *The New York Times*, October 20, 2012.

16. Ibid.

17. Jon Dalton and Pamela Crosby, "Challenging College Students to Learn in Campus Cultures of Comfort, Convenience and Complacency," *Journal of College and Character*, Vol. 9, 2008, pp. 1–5.

18. Jim Rohn, "Why Personal Development is Critical to Success," *Success Magazine*, May 17, 2015.

19. Seth Godin, *The Icarus Deception*, Penguin Books, New York City, NY, 2012.

20. Mark Gilman, "College Graduates: You're Doing It Wrong, and It's OK," *Huffington Post Blog*, May 22, 2013.

21. Ibid.

22. Thor Muller, "How to get lunch: making serendipity work for your career," CNN, May 26, 2012.

23. Alexander Rice, "Incorporation of Chance into Career Development Theory and Research," *Journal of Career Development*, Vol. 4, 2014.

24. Elizabeth Black, "Career Considerations: Serendipity or Strategy?" *Association for Talent Development*, September 7, 2012.

25. Deborah G. Betsworth and Jo-Ida C. Hansen, "The Categorization of Serendipitous Career Development Events," *Journal of Career Assessment*, Vol. 4, Winter 1996, pp. 91–98.

26. Thor Muller, "How to Get Lucky: Making Serendipity Work for Your Career," *CNN*, May 26, 2012.

27. Kathleen E. Mitchell, Al S. Levin, and John D. Kumboltz, "Planned Happenstance: Construction Unexpected Career Opportunities," *Journal of Counseling & Development*, Vol. 77, Spring 1999, pp. 115-124.

28. Edward W. Lempinen, "Serendipity Can Be Crucial to Professional Success, Chemist Luis Echegoyen Tells SACNAS," *The American Association for the Advancement of Science*, August 30, 2011.

29. Ibid.

30. John C. Smart and Michael B. Paulsen, editors, *Higher Education: Handbook of Theory and Research*, Vol. 26, Springer Science and Business Media, 2011.

31. Carolyn Gregoire, "6 Reasons to Step Outside Your Comfort Zone," *Huffington Post,* September 29, 2014.

32. Melinda Beck, "Anxiety Can Bring Out the Best," *The Wall Street Journal*, June 18, 2012.

33. Alina Tugend, "Tiptoeing Out of One's Comfort Zone (and of Course, Back In)," *The New York Times*, February 11, 2011.

CHAPTER 6

Create Options

Introduction

On Saturday December 19, 2015 Kurt Masur, the music director emeritus of the New York Philharmonic, died at 88 years of age. Born in Brieg in the Silesian region of Germany (now Brzeg, Poland) his father was an engineer, and, at his pragmatic insistence, young Kurt studied to become an electrician.[1] But Kurt he also studied music, training as a pianist, organist, cellist and percussionist. Wanting to make the field his calling, he entered the National Music School in Breslau. But by the time he was 16, an inoperable tendon injury in his right hand had made performing impossible, and he chose to concentrate on conducting. As a result of the hand condition, Masur conducted without a baton throughout his career.[2] For over 40 years Masur had a successful career conducting various orchestras, most notably the New York Philharmonic. He did so by creating options for himself early in his life. He first created an option when his father suggested that he train to become an electrician. His calling was towards music, a passion that he discovered on his own. But Masur had to create another option once he learned of his inoperable tumor so he opted to conduct. His ability to create options allowed Masur to translate his calling and passion into a career. Author Michael Punke also created options for his career.

Punke wrote *The Revenant*, a 2002 book inspired by the life of frontiersman Hugh Glass. While it took over ten years for Hollywood to translate Punke's work into the big screen, Alejandro G. Iñárritu directed the 2015 picture starting Leonardo DiCaprio and Tom Hardy, the story of how Punke wrote the book serves as another example of a successful person learning to create options by engaging in subtle maneuvers. Punke grew up in Torrington, Wyoming where he and his brother engaged in various outdoor activities such as fishing, hunting, hiking, and mountain biking while growing up. He graduated George Washington University with a degree in International Affairs and then Cornell Law School where he focused on trade law and became Editor-in-Chief of the *Cornell International Law Journal*.[3] He worked as a government staffer for Senator Max Baucus (D-Montana), and served at the White House as Director for International Economic Affairs and was jointly appointed to the National Economic Council and the National Security Council. While working in Washington, D.C., Punke had a desire to write a political novel but nothing caught his interest. Once he came across the story of frontiersmen Hugh Glass however, he knew he discovered the topic for his novel. According to Tim Punke, Michael's brother, Michael "used to get up at five in the morning, go into work and write for three hours, and then he do his job for eight or ten hours."[4] The book took four years to complete and the final year was particularly intense as Punke caught pneumonia four times finishing the novel.[5] While working a full-time job Punke engaged in subtle maneuvers for four years until he completed his novel. Although initial sales were disappointing, Punke sold the movie rights to his book in 2001 to producer Akiva Goldsman and 14 years later *The Revenant* was launched as a major motion picture directed by Alejandro G. Iñárritu starring Tom Hardy and Leonardo DiCaprio.[6] By creating options for themselves and looking beyond traditional career paths, both Masur and Punke demonstrated are two of the main elements in what others have labeled a jungle gym approach to their career.

In her book *Lean In: Women, Work and the Will to Lead*, Sheryl Sandberg borrows a career development metaphor of the jungle gym from *Fortune* magazine editor Pattie Sellers. "People who view their careers as jungle gyms, rather than ladders," observed Sellers, "make sure that their vision is always peripheral so that they can see opportunities that come along—and swing to them."[7] Sandberg continued that thought and wrote "A jungle gym scramble is the best description of my career since I could never have connected the dots from where I started to where I am today."[8] The jungle gym metaphor offers a different approach to career development than the traditional corporate ladder for a variety of reasons:

- *Movement*: The jungle gym allows you to move up, down, and sideways, whereas the ladder allows you to move only up and down. Having the flexibility of a jungle gym is an absolute necessity in today's challenge job market.

- *Collaboration*: The jungle gym allows you to work with others, while the ladder only offers you the opportunity to walk over someone to get to the next step.
- *Foundation*: The jungle gym has a wide base and therefore allows for a stronger foundation as compared to the ladder that has two legs and is subject to wind, shifts in weight, or unpaved surfaces.
- *Achievement*: The jungle gym allows more than one person to sit at the top, while the ladder has room only for one person.

Creating options via the jungle gym is especially relevant for new college graduates who possess high expectations that their degree will result in an immediate dream job following graduation. The pursuit of a 'dream job' is "a recipe for disappointment."[9] To build their path around, over, and through their career jungle gym, individuals need to expand their employment options. In *What Colour is Your Parachute?* Richard Bolles concluded, "Even in tough times there are jobs to be had, but applicants have to work far harder to get an employer's attention. They need to market themselves better and consider a broader range of employers."[10] *Successful people create options by selecting the right choice versus the best one, turning a disadvantage into an advantage and engaging in subtle maneuvers.*

Decide Between Best versus Right

Successful people spend a good deal of time comparing their best option to the right one. This is an important stepping stone to use as people will often be blinded by the allure of the "best" of something instead of the "right" one. This is often the case with the selection of what college to attend or major to select. People believe that they need to go to the best school. The best school provides the best education and the best opportunities to get the best job for the best career to have the best life. Nothing could be further from the truth. Successful people know that identifying the right option, not the best one, is the stepping stone.

The latest research regarding this topic can be found in Malcolm Gladwell's book *David and Goliath: Underdogs, Misfits, and The Art of Battling Giants*, who noted: "We strive for the best and attach great importance to getting into the finest institutions we can. But rarely do we stop and consider whether the most prestigious of institutions is always in our best interest." That type of thinking can be applied to almost anything in life. When making a decision, are you focused on the best option or the right one? Do you have the self-awareness required to choose the right one? If there are advantages to going to the best school, are there disadvantages? If one has a critical eye and an open mind, there usually are. It is also important to remember that others will disagree with your view on what is the best option compared to the right one. The research on job satisfaction is a good example of this. Contrary to common belief, salary is seldom the best determining factor to job happiness.

In his 1967 publication, *The Motivation to Work*, Frederick Herzberg identified two different categories of factors affecting the motivation to work: hygiene and motivation. Hygiene factors include extrinsic factors like technical supervision, interpersonal relations, physical working conditions, salary, company policies and administrative practices, benefits, and job security. In comparison, motivation factors include intrinsic factors such as achievement, recognition and status, responsibility, challenging work, and advancement in the organization. Herzberg's theory postulates that only motivation factors have the potential of increasing job satisfaction. "The results indicate that the association between salary and job satisfaction is very weak. When employees are focused on external rewards, the effects of intrinsic motives on engagement are significantly diminished. This means that employees who are intrinsically motivated are three times more engaged than employees who are extrinsically motivated (such as by money). Quite simply, you're more likely to like your job if you focus on the work itself, and less likely to enjoy it if you're focused on money."[11]

Daniel Pink's *Drive: The Surprising Truth About What Motivates Us* makes the same observation. Although many people believe that the best way to motivate others is with external rewards like money, the reality is that high performance and satisfaction is rooted in the three elements of true motivation: autonomy, mastery, and purpose. If you think that the best job offer to accept is the one that offers the most money, ask yourself if that is the right opportunity for you at this point in time. When deciding between two job opportunities, remind yourself that effort can trump ability and that conventions are made to be challenged. What is right for you may not be for other people. The story of Mario Renato Capecchi provides a good example of how successful people decide between what is right versus what is best.

Mario Renato Capecchi is an Italian-born American molecular geneticist and Nobel Prize winner and distinguished professor of human genetics and biology at the University of Utah School of Medicine, which he joined in 1973. His life story provides a variety of examples of how professional development is linked to personal growth. Capecchi was born in the Italian city of Verona in 1937 as the only child of an abusive father (Luciano) and a caring mother (Lucy) who worked as a poet and antifascist campaigner. Lucy refused to marry Capecchi's father. When Capecchi was around three years of age, German officers arrested his mother and sent her to a concentration camp, leaving Capecchi to fend for himself. For a time he lived with a family friend but when money ran out to support him, and he refused to live with his father, young Capecchi found himself a street orphan at the age of four and a half.

Between the ages of four and a half and nine, Capecchi wandered around the streets of wartime Italy. As Tim Harford wrote in Adapt: Why Success Always Starts with Failure, "Mario survived on scraps, joined gangs and drifted in and out of orphanages, and eventually had to be hospitalized for a year probably due to typhoid." At nine years of age, after not seeing his mother for almost six years and being homeless for almost as long, Capecchi was reunited with her after she spent nearly 18 months looking for him. With the help of relatives in the United States, both Mario and Lucy left for America soon after they were reunited. With the support of relatives and friends in Pennsylvania, Capecchi enrolled in school and eventually graduated from George School, a Quaker boarding school in Bucks County. He then graduated from Antioch College in Ohio with a BS in chemistry and physics in 1961 when he was 24 years of age. Mario enrolled at MIT's graduate program to study physics and mathematics, but subsequently became interested in molecular biology and transferred to Harvard to join the lab of James

D. Watson, codiscoverer of the structure of DNA. Capecchi received his PhD in biophysics in 1967 under the tutelage of Watson.

From 1967 to 1973, Capecchi held various faculty positions at Harvard but grew increasingly alarmed at its results-driven environment. Despite objections from Watson, who once quipped, "Capecchi accomplished more as a graduate student than most scientists accomplish in a life time and that he would be fucking crazy to pursue his studies anywhere other than in the cutting-edge intellectual atmosphere of Harvard." Capecchi left Harvard to join a new department at the University of Utah. He believed that the short-term gratification environment at Harvard limited his ability to breathe if he was to do great work. Capecchi chose what was right for him, not what was best. Capecchi's life story also demonstrates another characteristic of successful people; he turned his disadvantage into an advantage.

Turn Your Disadvantage into an Advantage

Many things are possible when you are allowed to fail once, and twice, and to try again, to break through the barriers of disadvantage. In fact, the great personality theorist Alfred Adler believed that healthy living involves trying to strengthen shortcomings that may be stopping you from carrying out the life you've imagined for yourself. Rather than a liability, disadvantage (physical, mental, or psychological) is an advantage. It is an opening for self-improvement that develops and grows your life in deeply meaningful ways.[12] Alfred Adler's theory is at once a model of personality, a theory of psychopathology, and in many cases the foundation of a method for mind development and personal growth. Adler wrote, "Every individual represents a unity of personality and the individual then fashions that unity. The individual is thus both the picture and the artist. Therefore, if one can change one's concept of self, they can change the picture being painted." Political scientist Ivan Arreguín-Toft examined this very issue in his book *How the Weak Win Wars*.

Arreguín-Toft looked at every war fought over the past 200 years between strong and weak combatants. Using a David versus Goliath framework, Arreguín-Toft found that Goliaths won 71.5 percent of the battles he studied. He discovered the remarkable fact that in historical conflicts where one side was at least 10 times as powerful in military strength and population as its opponent, the weaker side prevailed almost a third of the time. Arreguín-Toft then examined the outcome of historical battles when the underdogs acknowledged their weakness and chose an unconventional strategy. He went back and reanalyzed his data. In those cases, David's winning percentage went from 28.5 percent to 63.6 percent! Arreguín-Toft concluded that underdogs are more likely to win when they turn their disadvantage into an advantage, choose an unconventional strategy, and decide not to play by Goliath's rules. The underdogs win "even when everything we think we know about power says they shouldn't."[13]

In *David and Goliath: Underdogs, Misfits and the Art of Battling Giants*, best-selling author Malcolm Gladwell recounts the story of David—the shepherd boy who was summoned by his people to defend King Saul's kingdom against the Philistines. According to Gladwell David was not the underdog in his historic battle against the six-foot–nine inch giant, Goliath. Essentially, Goliath was equipped for direct combat, in which he might have deflected strikes with his shield and delivered a stab with his spear, not an opponent whose chief weaponry consisted of a slingshot and stones. David's decision to fight with less armor and weaponry, as opposed to Goliath, granted him insurmountable speed and mobility. Additionally, "Goliath had as much chance against David," writes the historian, Robert Dohrenwend, "as any Bronze Age warrior with a sword would have had against an [opponent] armed with a .45 automatic pistol." David had brought a gun to a sword fight. He had recognized his disadvantage of size as an advantage of speed, mobility, and ability. Goliath, as Gladwell summarized, "was blind to his approach—and then he was down, too big, and slow and blurry-eyed to comprehend the way the tables had been turned." One does not, however, need to examine hundreds of historical battles to find examples of how successful people have turned their disadvantage into an advantage. Paul Orfalea and Derrick Coleman provide two excellent case studies of individuals who turned their disadvantage into an advantage.

Suffering from undiagnosed attention deficit hyper disorder and dyslexia throughout his childhood, Orfalea was a "C" student in college. He graduated from college with a degree in finance in 1971. It was difficult for him to hold a job, so he decided to start his own company to make money. He asked his father to cosign a loan for $5,000 and leased an 80-square-foot former hamburger stand in Isla Vista, near the campus of the University of California at Santa Barbara, and rented a small Xerox copier, charging customers four cents a page. He got the idea for a photocopy store from watching students make copies in the school library. His goal was to offer college students with products and services they needed at a competitive price. He named the store Kinko's after his curly red hair. The store also sold notebooks and pens, so he had to wheel the copier out on the sidewalk when the premises became too crowded. To supplement his income, Orfalea also went from one dormitory room to another in the evenings, hawking his wares from a knapsack.

When his first Kinko's proved a success, Orfalea decided to open stores on other college campuses. Lacking funds to finance them and having no desire to franchise, Orfalea opened new Kinko's on his ability to build relationships with others and formed partnerships with owner-operators, retaining a controlling interest in each. "These partners were other students who scouted locations along the West Coast, sleeping in their Volkswagen buses or fraternity houses. Publicity consisted of flyers stuffed in mailboxes; orders were taken and delivered personally." Due to his inability to read and write, he realized early on that to get through school he was going to need help from a lot of people. This dependence taught him how to ask for help. In turn, it also taught Orfalea how to provide what help he could to others. He "learned to appreciate people's strengths and forgive their weaknesses, as he hoped they would forgive his." In a recent study examining dyslexics who ventured into entrepreneurship, it was suggested that "strategies they have used since childhood to offset their weaknesses in written communication and organizational ability—identifying trustworthy people and handing over major responsibilities to them—can be applied to businesses and gives them a significant advantage over non-dyslexic entrepreneurs, who tend to like to be in total control." Orfalea turned his entrepreneurial vision into a $2 billion-a-year company with more than 1,500 branches and 21,000 coworkers worldwide. In 2004, Kinko's was acquired by the FedEx Corporation.

The first deaf player in NFL history was defensive tackle Bonnie Sloan, a 1973 member of the St. Louis Cardinals who thought it was fortuitous that he did not have to hear his coach curse. The second was defensive end Kenny Walker, a Denver Broncos 1991 draft pick out of Nebraska, who was so thorough he used to bring an interpreter with him to team meetings.

But the third deaf NFL player has gone where none has ever gone before . . . to offense, where, in the 21st century there are audibles and "Omaha's" and outright races to the line of scrimmage to snap the football.[14] Derrick Coleman, a backup fullback for the Seahawks, is overwhelmed by none of it.[15]

When he is in the lineup, the first person he finds is quarterback Russell Wilson. He follows Wilson to the huddle. He asks Wilson to stare at him during the play call. If there's an audible under center, he expects Wilson to turn around and mouth it to him loud and clear. If Wilson forgets, he'll go grab the quarterback's face mask. That's his other survival skill: whatever it takes.[16] It's simple, actually: You don't have to hear to be able to listen As fellow dyslexic Richard Branson said "Whatever personal challenge you have to overcome, you must be brave enough to accept that you are different. You must have the courage to trust your instincts and be ready to question what other people don't. If you do that, you can seize opportunities that others would miss. Believe in yourself, and use everything you can—including the obstacles—to propel you along the road to success. Who knows what you might achieve?"[17]

Engage in Subtle Maneuvers

David Ferguson wrote an article in the satirical publication *The Onion* entitled "Find the Thing You're Most Passionate About, Then Do It on Nights and Weekends for The Rest of Your Life" in March 2013.[18] But that satirical statement is actually how many successful people approach their life. Jon Acuff's book, *Quitter: Closing the Gap Between Your Day Job & Your Dream Job*, examines the possibility and reality of translating an idea for a new product or service into a dream and not a nightmare while balancing the demands of a full-time employment position. Mason Currey's book, *Daily Rituals: How Artists Work*, examines dozens of creative people and concludes that most of them engaged in subtle maneuvers to pursue meaningful creative work while also earning a living.[19]

"The book makes one thing abundantly clear: There's no such thing as the way to create good work, but all greats have their way."[20] An aspiring author once wrote to Irish playwright Oscar Wilde, asking for advice on how to have a success career as a writer. In his response, Wilde told him not to rely on earning a living from writing and declared that "the best work in literature is always done by those who do not depend on it for their daily bread."[21]

Most people would complain that they do not have enough time. As author H. Jackson Brown, Jr. said "Don't say you don't have enough time. You have exactly the same number of hours per day that were given to Helen Keller, Pasteur, Michaelangelo, Mother Teresa, Leonardo da Vinci, Thomas Jefferson, and Albert Einstein." How you leverage your time matters. One of the strategies that successful people have used throughout history and into the present day is the ability to engage in subtle maneuvers. When you are pressed for time, recall the words of Franz Kafka to his finance: "Time is short, my strength is limited, the office is a horror, the apartment is noisy, and if a pleasant, straightforward life is not possible, then one must try to wriggle through by subtle maneuvers."[22] During the day, Kafka worked his *brotberuf*, literally "bread job," a job done only to pay the bills, at an insurance company and then he would pursue his passion of writing at night and during the weekend. This subtle maneuver approach has been utilized by many successful people.

Pulitzer Prize winning poet Wallace Stevens, an American Modernist poet, engaged in subtle maneuvers. After a brief career in law, Stevens joined the home office of The Hartford Accident and Indemnity Company in 1916. With a love of writing poetry dating back to his undergraduate days at Harvard University, Stevens started to write at nights and on weekends. By 1934, he had been named vice president of the company. Stevens's first book of poetry, *Harmonium*, was published in 1923. He would go on to produce additional works throughout the 1920s and into the 1940s. He won the Pulitzer Prize for Poetry for his Collected Poems in 1955. After he won the Pulitzer Prize in 1955, he was offered a faculty position at Harvard but declined since it would have required him to give up his vice presidency of The Hartford.[23] William Faulkner wrote *As I Lay Dying* in the afternoons before clocking in on the night shift as a supervisor at a university power plant. He found the nocturnal schedule easy enough to manage. After sleeping for a few hours in the morning, he would write during the afternoon and then visit his mother on the way to work. He would often nap due to the undemanding nature of his work. The novelist Henry Green was independently wealthy and did not need to work. Since he liked the structure of an office job, he went into his family's manufacturing business every day. Joseph Heller thrived in magazine advertising by day and wrote *Catch-22* in the evenings, sitting at the kitchen table in his Manhattan apartment. According to Heller, "I spent two or three hours a night on it for eight years. . . . I gave up once and started watching television with my wife. Television drove me back to *Catch-22*."[24] The American composer Charles Ives never let music get too far from his mind. After graduating from Yale in 1898, he secured a position in New York as a $15-a-week clerk with the Mutual Life Insurance Company.[25] Though already an accomplished and talented organist as well as composer, he was looking to create beyond the conservative musical establishment of his day. So staying in a steady job made sense. As Ives put it, if a composer "has a nice wife and some nice children, how can he let them starve on his dissonances?"[26]

Robert Frost was changing light bulb filaments in a Massachusetts factory when he sold his first poem, "*My Butterfly: An Elegy*" in 1894. Kurt Vonnegut managed a Saab dealership on Cape Cod after he'd published his first novel *Player Piano*. Charlotte Brontë worked as a poorly paid governess who had to pay her employers out of her own pocket for using their facilities to wash her clothes. Poet William Carlos Williams was a career pediatrician in New Jersey, working long hours caring for patients and penning phrases on the back of prescription slips. Musician Philip Glass worked as a plumber, furniture mover, and taxi driver. Such jobs were integral to his artistic process. According to Glass, "I was careful to take a job that couldn't have any possible meaning for me." He never earned a living from his music until he was 42.[27] How did these individuals accomplish so much while working a day job? As one observer noted, "you find out a way to get more done when you're really busy. You just learn how to fit it in."[28] Every now and then, a subtle maneuver sparks a much larger movement with very positive results without any intention of doing so in the first place. One such example is Tippi Hedren.

Hedren played a role in the development of Vietnamese-American nail salons in the United States. In 1975, while an international relief coordinator with Food for the Hungry, she began visiting with refugees at Hope Village outside Sacramento, CA. When Hedren found that the women were interested in her manicured nails, she employed her manicurist to teach them the skills of the trade and worked with a local beauty school to help them find jobs. Vietnamese-Americans now dominate the multibillion dollar nail salon business in North America. That actress was Tippi Hedren, an elegant blond who starred in several of Alfred Hitchcock's movies in the 1960s. When she wasn't onscreen, Hedren was an international relief coordinator with the organization Food for the Hungry. After Saigon fell, she was working with Vietnamese women in a refugee camp near Sacramento when several admired her long, glossy nails. Hedren had a manicurist named Dusty at the time and asked her if she would come to the camp to meet with the women. Dusty agreed, and Hedren flew her up to Camp Hope every weekend to teach nail technology to 20 eager women. Hedren also flew in seamstresses and typists all in the name of helping "find vocations for the Vietnamese women."[29] Hedren also recruited a local beauty school to help teach the women. When they graduated, Hedren helped get the women jobs all over Southern California. Those 20 women—mainly the wives of high-ranking military officers and at least one woman who worked in military intelligence—went on to transform the industry, which is now worth about $8 billion and is dominated by Vietnamese-Americans.[30]

Conclusion

Successful people create options by selecting the right choice versus the best one, turning a disadvantage into an advantage, and engaging in subtle maneuvers. When Steve Jobs was launching iTunes, Apple only had around two percent of the personal computer market. While two percent market share might be interpreted as a disadvantage for many people, Jobs thought otherwise. He turned his disadvantage into an advantage when he convinced music executives to license music on Apple's terms as an experiment. After all, with just two percent of the personal computer market, what did the music industry have to lose?[31] Such a move allowed Steve Jobs to create an entirely new way people purchased, stored, and listened to music. Creating options is a critical factor in order for people to succeed in today's ever changing world.

In today's volatile, uncertain, chaotic, and ambiguous global marketplace where change is constant and competition grows fiercer every day, successful people rely on their ability to create options to survive the chaos. In *The Chaos Theory of Careers: A New Perspective on Working in the Twenty-First Century*, Robert Pryor and Jim Bright discuss the chaos theory of career development that offers individuals a blank slate upon which to transform their current self to their possible self, but this ability to transform one's current self to a possible self requires positive uncertainty. To deal with positive uncertainty, which involves complexity, change, and chance, H.B. Gelatt identified four major paradoxes that successful people understand as they move forward in their career decision-making process:

- Be focused and flexible about what you want.
- Be aware and wary about what you know.
- Be objective and optimistic about what you believe.
- Be practical and magical about what you do.

Positive uncertainty is compatible with the new science and beliefs of today's society and incompatible with yesterday's decision dogma. It involves ambiguity and paradox because the future is full of ambiguity and paradox. In the future, it will help to realize that one does not know some things, cannot always see what is coming, and frequently will not be able to control it. Successful people remain positive amidst the uncertainty in order to create options as it allows them to act when one is uncertain about what they are doing.

Questions and resources for characteristic #6: Create options

Reading list

- Richard Wiseman, *The Luck Factor: The Four Essential Principles*
- Robert Pryor and Jim Bright, *The Chaos Theory of Careers: A New Perspective on Working in the Twenty-First Century*
- Sheryl Sandberg, *Lean In: Women, Work and the Will to Lead*
- Malcolm Gladwell, *David and Goliath: Underdogs, Misfits and the Art of Battling Giants*
- Ivan Arreguin-Toft, *How the Weak Win Wars: A Theory of Asymmetric Conflict*
- Malcolm Gladwell's book *David and Goliath: Underdogs, Misfits, and The Art of Battling Giants*
- Jon Acuff, *Quitter: Closing the Gap Between Your Day Job & Your Dream Job*
- Mason Currey, *Daily Rituals: How Artists Work*

Questions

- Do you believe luck is the intersection of where opportunity meets preparedness?
- Do you find yourself suggesting that others got lucky and that is why they have succeeded?
- Have you ever been lucky?
- What have you done recently to change your luck?
- Have you played a role in anyone's luck?
- Do you feel as though you have any career options at this point in time?
- What have you done to create options for yourself lately?
- When were you able to generate options for yourself in the past?
- Have you helped anyone else understand they have options?
- Why do you think people have a difficult time creating options?
- Have you ever turned a disadvantage into an advantage?
- How do you respond when you find yourself in a situation where you are at a disadvantage?

- Have you helped others turn their disadvantage into an advantage?
- Have you had to believe in yourself when others did not believe in your ability?
- Has your advantage ever been a disadvantage to you?

There's almost nothing you can't learn your way out of. Life is like jail with an unlocked, heavy door. You're free the minute you realize the door will open if you simply lean into it.

—Scott Adams (creator of Dilbert)

Endnotes

1. Margalit Fox, "Kurt Masur dies at 88; Conductor Transformed New York Philharmonic," *The New York Times*, December 19, 2015.

2. Ibid.

3. Walter Bonner, "'The Revenant' author Michael Punke is the most successful novelist who can't talk about his book," *Maxim*, November 11, 2014.

4. Ibid.

5. Ben Terris, "Meet the author of 'The Revenant'—except you can't because of his federal job," *Washington Post*, December 22, 2015.

6. Ibid.

7. Patricia Sellers, "Power Point: Get used to the jungle gym," *Fortune*, August 7, 2009.

8. Deborah L. Jacobs, "Why a Career Jungle Gym Is Better than a Career Ladder," *Forbes*, March 14, 2013.

9. Lisa Wade, "Two-Thirds of College Students Think They're Going to Change the World," *The Society Pages*, May 20, 2013.

10. "My Big Fat Career," *The Economist*, September 10, 2011.

11. Tomas Chamorro-Premuzic, "Does Money Really Affect Motivation? A Review of the Research," *Harvard Business Review*, April 10, 2013.

12. Deborah Khoshaba, "When Disadvantage Is Your Advantage," *Psychology Today*, April 27, 2013.

13. Ivan Arreguin-Toft, *How the Weak Win Wars: A Theory of Asymmetric Conflict*, New York, Cambridge University Press, 2005.

14. Tom Friend, "Derrick Coleman Misses Nothing," *ESPN*, January 31, 2014.

15. Ibid.

16. For more information see Derrick Coleman Jr., *No Excuses: Growing Up Deaf and Achieving My Super Bowl Dreams*, New York City, NY, Gallery Books, 2015.

17. Richard Branson, "Richard Branson on Turning a Disadvantage to Your Advantage," *Entrepreneur*, August 19, 2012.

18. David Ferguson, "Find the Thing You're Most Passionate About, Then Do It on Nights and Weekends for the Rest of Your Life," *The Onion*, March 20, 2013.

19. Mason Currey, *Daily Rituals: How Artists Work,* New York, Knopf, 2013.

20. John Wilwol, *Daily Rituals,' of the Brilliantly Creative*, NPR Books, 2013.

21. Nadia Khomami, "Literary Success? Don't Give up the Day Job, Advised Oscar Wilde," *The Telegraph,* March 19, 2013.

22. Mason Currey, *Daily Rituals: How Artists Work*, New York, Alfred A. Knopf, 2013, p. 83.

23. Wikipedia, "Wallace Stevens," https://en.wikipedia.org/wiki/Wallace_Stevens (accessed August 15, 2015).

24. Mason Currey, "Daily Rituals," *Slate*, May 2, 2013.

25. Lydia Dishman, "10 Famous Creative Minds That Didn't Quit Their Day Jobs," *Fast Company*, December 6, 2013.

26. Gayle Sherwood Magee, *Charles Ives Reconsidered*, Urbana, IL, University of Illinois Press, 2008.

27. Lydia Dishman, "10 Famous Creative Minds That Didn't Quit Their Day Jobs," *Fast Company*, December 6, 2013.

28. Mason Currey, "Daily Rituals," *Slate*, May 2, 2013.

29. Regan Morris, "How Tippi Hedren Made Vietnamese Refugees into Nail Salon Magnates," *BBC Magazine*, May 3, 2015.

30. Ibid.

31. David B. Yoffie and Michael A. Cusumano, interviewed by Martha E. Mangelsdorf, "Mastering Strategy," *MIT Sloan Management Review,* Winter 2016.

CHAPTER 7

Maintain a High Level of Energy

Introduction

Successful people maintain a high level of energy. In July 2009 Ursula M. Burns became the CEO of Xerox and in so doing became the first black-American woman CEO to head a Fortune 500 company. Her success required a high level of energy as she was raised by a single mother who was a Panamanian immigrant in the Baruch Houses, a New York City housing project. "Her mom scraped together enough funds from doing domestic work to send her daughter to Catholic high school."[1] Burns obtained a Bachelor of Science degree in Mechanical Engineering from New York University Polytechnic School of Engineering in 1980 and a Master of Science in Mechanical Engineering from Columbia University. In a June 7, 2015 Commencement speech at Williams College, Burns discussed how being poor, black, and a woman did not deter her.[2] With her mother's guidance, a fierce determination to succeed, and a high level of energy, Burns achieved tremendous success and in 2014 *Forbes* rated her the 22nd most powerful woman in the world.[3] While not one of the most powerful people in the world, cartoonist Scott Adams relied on his high level of energy to create a recognizable brand in Dilbert.

Scott Adams wanted to be a cartoonist since he was six years old when he would read old Peanuts collections at his uncle's farm. Those drawings eventually made their way into his business presentations. One of his coworkers suggested that Adams call his one character Dilbert. So Dilbert would have a companion, he created Dogbert as well. With a character in hand and a belief that he had the ability to create his own life, Adams sought the advice of cartoonist Jack Cassady on how to get syndicated. Adams drew 50 sample cartoon strips and mailed copies to various cartoon syndicates. Within a few weeks, United Media called and offered him a contract and launched Dilbert in 1989. It would, however, be another six years before Adams could quit his day job. From 1989 until 1995, he created Dilbert during mornings, evenings, and weekends while maintaining his full-time job. Throughout his life, Adams has relied on using affirmations to help him believe he creates his own life. He has written often about his practice and belief in writing your goals down 15 times each day. In his 2013 book *How to Fail at Almost Everything and Still Win Big: Kind of the Story of My Life*, Adams highlights two important aspects of his success: "Good ideas have no value because the world already has too many of them. The market rewards execution, not ideas;" and "Goals are for losers. Focus on the process."[4] *Successful people maintain a high level of energy by managing their fear, learning deep survival tactics, and performing under pressure.*

Manage Your Fear

In the 2005 American romantic comedy and drama film *The Upside of Anger* Evan Rachel Wood's character Lavender "Popeye" Wolfmeyer said "Anger and resentment can stop you in your tracks. It can change you, turn you, mold you and shape you into something you're not. The only upside to anger, then is the person you become."[5] Recognizing what so many successful people have been able to do, she finished her thought by stating "Hopefully the person you become is someone who wakes up one day and realizes they're not afraid to take the journey . . . and that anger leaves a new chance at acceptance, and the promise of calm in its wake."[6] Rick Allen and Arthur Boorman are two examples of people who did not allow anger or fear to stop them in their tracks.

After joining the rock band Def Leppard at age 15, Rick Allen got into a car accident six years later, which resulted in the amputation of his left arm. Unable to play the drums, Allen sunk into a state of depression and feared that he would never again play drums. Thanks to Def Leppard's lead singer Joe Elliott, and with the help of others, Allen managed his fear and learned how to play a newly designed drum set with his feet and right arm. Two years after his accident, Allen was back playing with the band.[7] Allen noted that "taking risks always comes with a fear of failure or rejection for me but when I trust my true potential I am able to push through my fear and follow my heart. Before I sat behind the drum kit my head told me I was defeated and not even to try but my heart knew better. With the help of people around me saying I could, and by using my creativity in creating a way to play with my feet, I was able to take a chance to achieve what may have been impossible."[8] Allen's approach to recovering from this accident and mastering his fear symbolizes Eleanor Roosevelt's belief that "You gain strength, courage, and confidence by every experience in which you really stop to look fear in the face. You must do the thing which you think you cannot do." Arthur Boorman, much like Allen, learned to manage his fear in order to move forward.

Boorman served as a paratrooper and sustained injuries that left him unable to walk without the aid of crutches or canes. For 15 years physicians told him that he would never walk unassisted again. His fear of never being able to walk unassisted molded him into something he was not accustomed to: a depressed, sad, and overweight person. Boorman's weight eventually ballooned over 300 pounds. One day while surfing on the internet he stumbled upon the *Yoga for Regular Guys* DVDs by Diamond Dallas Page.[9] He immediately connected with the style of yoga and spent the next ten months managing his fear and practicing as much yoga as possible. He would ultimately lost 140 pounds and gain his yoga teacher certification. To record his progress his son Warren created a video "Never, Ever Give Up. Arthur's Inspirational Transformation!"[10] They uploaded Arthur's story in 2012 and it went viral as one of the most inspirational videos that year. As of December 2015 over 12 million people watched Arthur's transformation from an overweight veteran unable to walk unassisted to an active yogi and runner. Recognizing how difficult his transformation was, Arthur mentioned in an interview that "a lot of people contact me looking for some magic pill to help them get motivated to lose weight but there is no such thing."[11] Both Boorman and Allen learned to manage their fear in order to transform their lives.

Mark Twain noted one of the most important stepping stones to success in his statement on fear: "Courage is resistance to fear, mastery of fear—not absence of fear." Rare is the successful person who has a life free of fear. Joseph LeDoux, professor of neuroscience and psychology in the Center for the Neuroscience of Fear and Anxiety based at New York University, defined fear as the "response to the immediate stimuli. The empty feeling in your gut, the racing of your heart, palms sweating, the nervousness—that's your brain responding in a preprogrammed way to a very specific threat."[12] As identified in the Chapman University Survey of American Fears, a random sampling of 1,541 American adults in April 2015, there are 10 major domains of fear with corresponding secondary domains. See the table below for a list of the domains.[13]

Primary domain	Secondary domain
Crime	Murder, rape, theft, burglary, fraud, identity theft
Daily life	Romantic rejection, ridicule, talking to strangers
Environment	Global warming, overpopulation, pollution
Government	Government corruption, Obamacare, drones, gun control, immigration issues
Judgment of others	Appearance, weight, age, race
Man-made disasters	Biowarfare, terrorism, nuclear attacks
Natural disasters	Earthquakes, droughts, floods, hurricanes
Personal anxieties	Tight spaces, public speaking, clowns, vaccines
Personal future	Dying, illness, running out of money, unemployment
Technology	Artificial intelligence, robots, cyberterrorism

Researchers have examined each one of these primary and secondary domains and continue to discover fascinating links between fears and success. One such researcher was Daniel Gardner who published *The Science of Fear: Why We Fear the Things We Shouldn't—and Put Ourselves in Greater Danger*. Gardner examined cancer, how the media sells fear, the economy, and a host of other topics. Gardner opens up his book by highlighting research conducted on the travel patterns of Americans following the September 11, 2001, terrorist attacks. The official death toll for the September 11 attacks stands at 2,996, including the 19 hijackers, but research suggests that there is a further, indirect toll as a result of behavioral changes induced by fear.[14] In the months after the 2001 terror attacks, passenger miles on the main U.S. airlines fell between 12% and 20%, while road use increased. The change is widely believed to have been caused by concerned passengers opting to drive rather than fly. Travelling long distances by car is more dangerous than travelling the same distance by plane. Measuring the exact effect is complex because there is no way of knowing for sure what the trends in road travel would have been had 9/11 not happened. Gardner included the work of Professor Gerd Gigerenzer, a German academic specializing in risk, in his publication. Gigerenzer estimated that an extra 1,595 Americans died in car accidents in the year after the attacks—indirect victims of the tragedy. He used trends in road and air use to suggest that, for a period of about 12 months, there was a temporary increase in road use before citizens again became more willing to fly at similar rates to before the attacks. Gigerenzer ascribed the extra deaths to people's poor understanding of danger. "People jump from the frying pan into the fire.[15]

Learn Deep Survival Tactics

When confronted with a life-threatening situation, 90 percent of people freeze or panic while the remaining 10 percent stay cool, focused, and alive. In *Deep Survival: Who Lives, Who Dies and Why*, Laurence Gonzales uncovers the biological and psychological reasons people risk their lives and why some are better at it than others. In the first part of the book, the author talks to dozens of thrill-seekers—mountain climbers, sailors, jet pilots—and they all say the same thing: danger is a great rush. "Fear can be fun," Gonzales writes. "It can make you feel more alive, because it is an integral part of saving your own life." To explain why and how those 10 percent lived, Gonzales identified 12 traits that disaster survivors have in common:[16]

- Perceive opportunity in the situation
- Stay calm
- Set up small manageable tasks
- Convert thoughts to action
- Celebrate successes
- Count your blessings
- Play
- Appreciate
- Believe success is possible

- Let go of fear
- Do whatever is necessary
- Never give up

In his follow-up publication, Gonzales wrote *Surviving Survival: The Art and Science of Resilience* and examines the role of fear, courage, and adaptability of the human spirit in the aftermath of a life-threatening situation. In some cases, survivors suffer more in the aftermath than they did during the actual crisis. In all cases, they have to work hard to reinvent themselves. One such person that had to reinvent himself was Dr. Francisco Bucio.

Dr. Francisco Bucio practiced the deep survival tactics to overcome the obstacle of a near-death experience that threatened his ability to perform surgery. On September 19, 1985, the young doctor's world shattered into pieces as one of the largest earthquakes in Mexican history, measuring 8.1 on the Richter Scale, hit Mexico City and killed more than 5,000 people.[17] Dr. Bucio was on the hospital's fifth floor when the earthquake hit. When the earthquake stopped, Dr. Bucio found himself on the ground floor buried under debris and surrounded by darkness. Eventually, rescue workers found Bucio buried in the rubble, but his hand was stuck so much that they wanted to cut it off so they could free him.

Realizing his dream to be a surgeon, his family asked the workers to do everything they can to free Bucio without cutting off his hand. It would take four days but the workers eventually got him out of the building and saved his hand. When Bucio arrived at the hospital, however, doctors realized that there was so much nerve damage that they were forced to amputate four fingers, leaving only his thumb. Realizing his dream would be lost if he could not use both his hands, Bucio set out to find someone to help. He found what he was looking for when he met Dr. Harry Buncke, Chief of Microsurgery at Davies Medical Center in San Francisco. In December 1985, Dr. Buncke and a surgical team removed Bucio's second toes, complete with arteries, tendons, and nerves and attached the toes to the stump of the sheared hand as the ring and pinkie fingers.[18]

For the next several months, Bucio demonstrated the highest level of self-discipline as he underwent intense rehabilitation. He believed he would succeed and swam to build up his endurance. He never gave up and practiced typing to strengthen his hand. He did whatever was necessary, including learning how to tie knots and dice food into small pieces. He even taught himself to become ambidextrous so that he could rely on his left hand more. Six weeks after the surgery, he was able to sign his name. His disciplined approach to therapy allowed him to return to Mexico City and go back to work at the hospital again. Initially, he performed minor tasks but over time was able to assist in operations. Dr. Francisco Bucio is currently a board-certified plastic surgeon in Tijuana, Mexico. Bucio practiced the deep survival tactics to live the life he envisioned by learning how to manage his stress in such a traumatic situation.

Researchers and psychologists are now postulating that individuals can learn to identify and manage reactions to stress. Stanford University health psychologist Kelly McGonigal wrote *The Upside of Stress: Why Stress is Good for You, and How to Get Good at It* and declared that people can develop healthier outlooks as well as improve performance on cognitive tests, at work, and in competition. Stress can either be beneficial (adaptive) or harmful (threatening) according to the latest research. With beneficial or adaptive stress, the sympathetic nervous system and the hypothalamus, pituitary, and adrenal glands pump stress hormones, adrenaline, and cortisol, into the bloodstream while heartbeat and breathing speed up, and muscles tense. [19] According to research by Wendy Mendes, an associate professor in the department of psychiatry at the University of California, San Francisco, and others, people experiencing beneficial stress feel pumped, their blood vessels dilate, and have an increase in blood flow to help the brain, muscles, and limbs meet a challenge. The body, however, tends to respond differently under harmful or threatening stress. Christopher Edwards, director of the behavioral chronic pain management program at Duke University Medical Center, suggests that the blood vessels constrict, and "you may feel a little dizzy as your blood pressure rises."[20] "Stress is a very healthy thing, because it gives you the energy you need to live life," says Jacob Teitelbaum, MD, medical director of the national fibromyalgia and fatigue centers and chronicity and author of Real Cause, Real Cure. "Without it, you wouldn't have the energy you need to take action."[21]

Harvard Business School professor Alison Wood Brooks designed an experiment to find out if telling people to calm down during a stressful moment was beneficial. In her research paper "Get Excited: Reappraising

Pre-Performance Anxiety as Excitement," published in the *Journal of Experimental Psychology*, she recruited 140 people to give a speech. She told part of the group to relax and repeat the phrase "I am calm," while the others were told to embrace their anxiety and tell themselves, "I am excited." Members of both groups were still nervous before the speech, but the participants who had told themselves "I am excited" felt better able to handle the pressure, were more confident of their ability to give a compelling talk, and received higher approval ratings from the audience. The excited speakers were found to be more persuasive, confident, and competent than the participants who had tried to calm down. By changing the mindset just slightly, from "calm down" to "I am excited," the speakers had transformed their anxiety into energy that helped them to perform under pressure.[22] "Individuals can reappraise anxiety as excitement using minimal strategies such as self-talk (e.g., saying "I am excited" out loud) or simple messages (e.g., "get excited"), which lead them to feel more excited, adopt an opportunity mind-set (as opposed to a threat mind-set), and improve their subsequent performance."[23]

Perform Under Pressure

Today's technological revolution continues to increase the perceived pressure in our lives. The continued global financial crisis, geopolitical instability, and the fierce competition for jobs around the world are just a few of the many critical issues facing the world today. These and other issues continue to place individuals under varying degrees of stress. Whether one wants to graduate college, identify a new employment position, find a romantic partner, improve their golf swing, or succeed at just about anything else that creates stress in the cerebral or physical context, there is substantial new research on performing under pressure. Sian Beilock, Ph.D., is an associate professor of psychology at the University of Chicago and an expert on the brain science behind "choking under pressure." In her book *Choke: What the Secrets of the Brain Reveal About Getting It Right When You Have To,* Beilock suggests that choking can occur when people think too much about activities that are usually automatic and suffer from "paralysis by analysis." Unfortunately, people also choke under pressure when they are not devoting enough attention to what they are doing and rely on simple or incorrect routines. For Beilock, her research suggests the following:

- Choking is not a lifetime curse. You can train, even hardwire, your brain to react more productively.
- Experience at performing under pressure makes a significant difference. Practicing under even mild pressure helps prepare you for the more intense version of a championship-winning or match-winning putt.
- When you're faced with a pressure shot, distracting yourself from the task at hand is helpful.
- Performing quickly in pressure situations leads to more success.

Two other publications have also examined performing under pressure. In their book, *Performing Under Pressure: The Science of Doing Your Best When It Matters Most*, Hendrie Weisinger and J.P. Pawliw-Fry concluded that "the difference between regular people and ultra-successful people is not that the latter group thrives under pressure. It's that they're better able to mitigate its negative effects." During the years of research, Weisinger and Pawliw-Fry found that pressure adversely impacts our cognitive success, pressure downgrades our behavioral skills, most people perform below their capability while under pressure, and pressure is often camouflaged. Moreover, Paul Sullivan's work *Clutch: Excel Under Pressure* highlights five key traits of clutch performers who succeeded under pressure: focus, discipline, adaptability, being truly present, and having the fear and desire to win. Through vignettes of accomplished professionals across a wide spectrum of interests, Sullivan provides examples of individuals who demonstrated the traits required to succeed under pressure.

Professor Geir Jordet from the Norwegian School of Sports Sciences examined the pressure that soccer players face during penalty shots. Jordet examined the film footage of almost 400 kicks from penalty shootouts during major tournaments and found that players need to take their time. Using the film footage, Jordet timed exactly how long players took to place the ball on the penalty spot. Those who took less than a second scored 58 percent of the time, compared with 80 percent when they didn't rush it and took longer than a second.[24] Adjusting to the pressure of a penalty shot takes time, so players who adapt practice that habit.

Conclusion

Successful people maintain a high level of energy by managing their fear, learning deep survival tactics, and performing under pressure. Maintaining a high level of energy is imperative in today's stressful environment fueled by ubiquitous technology that often contributes to burnout. According to research conducted by the American Psychological Association, in its annual *Stress in America* survey, Americans' stress levels are indeed trending downward. "The average reported stress level is 4.9 on a 10-point scale, down from 6.2 in 2007. Regardless of lower stress levels, it appears that Americans are living with stress levels higher than what we believe to be healthy—3.7 on a 10-point scale—and some (22 percent) say they are not doing enough to manage their stress."[25] One of the byproducts of stress is burnout. The Association of Psychology Science identified three types of burnout:

- *Overload*: The frenetic employee who works toward success until exhaustion, is most closely related to emotional venting. These individuals might try to cope with their stress by complaining about the organizational hierarchy at work, feeling as though it imposes limits on their goals and ambitions. That coping strategy, unsurprisingly, seems to lead to a stress overload and a tendency to throw in the towel.
- *Lack of Development*: Most closely associated with an avoidance coping strategy. These under challenged workers tend to manage stress by distancing themselves from work, a strategy that leads to depersonalization and cynicism—a harbinger for burning out and packing up shop.
- *Neglect*: Seems to stem from a coping strategy based on giving up in the face of stress. Even though these individuals *want* to achieve a certain goal, they lack the motivation to plow through barriers to get to it.

Ron Friedman, author of *The Best Place to Work: The Art and Science of Creating an Extraordinary Workplace*, concludes that individuals are at greater risk of burnout today than 10 years ago because people are surrounded by devices designed to distract people and make everything feel urgent. Heidi Grant Halvorson, a social psychologist and the author of *No One Understands You and What to Do About It*, agrees with Friedman. Halvorson suggests that there is a lot of pressure in today's 24/7 always on cycle and it can leave people feeling lethargic, stressed, and depleted, and called for people to find new ways to maintain a high level of energy.[26] Successful people understand that maintaining a high level of energy is often associated with interesting work and engaging relationships. Recent research from Duke University suggests that the level of interest in daily tasks is linked to how well people performed them. Not only does interest maximize performance, it also acts as a buffer against burning out.[27]

Questions and resources for characteristic #7: Maintain a high level of energy

Reading list

- *The Science of Fear: Why We Fear the Things We Shouldn't—and Put Ourselves in Greater Danger*
- Laurence Gonzales *Deep Survival: Who Lives, Who Dies and Why*
- Laurence Gonzales, *Surviving Survival: The Art and Science of Resilience*
- Kelly McGonigal, *The Upside of Stress: Why Stress is Good for You, and How to Get Good at It*
- *Performing Under Pressure: The Science of Doing Your Best When It Matters Most*
- Sian Beilock, *Choke: What the Secrets of the Brain Reveal About Getting It Right When You Have To*
- Paul Sullivan, *Clutch: Excel Under Pressure*

Questions

- How often do you find yourself managing your fear?
- Has fear stopped you from making progress toward a goal?
- Have you allowed fear to dictate or contribute to a major life decision?
- When is the last time you assessed your relationship to fear?
- Have you asked anyone to help you manage your fear?
- Have you helped anyone manage their fear?
- Why do you think fear stops people from making progress toward their goal?
- Have you survived a near-death experience?
- Have you demonstrated any of the 12 survival tactics Gonzales identified?
- Have you helped anyone recover from their life-threatening experience?
- How can you apply one or more of the survival tactics to everyday life as you work toward a personal or professional goal?

You have to exercise rebellion: to refuse to tape yourself to rules, to see every day, every year, every idea as a true challenge - and then you are going to live your life on a tightrope.

—Philippe Petit

Endnotes

1. Jessica Shambora, "Xerox's next CEO: Ursula Burns," *Fortune*, May 22, 2009.

2. Williams College Commencement speaker Xerox CEO Ursula M. Burns, June 7, 2015.

3. Jessica Shambora, "Xerox's next CEO: Ursula Burns," *Fortune*, May 22, 2009.

4. Scott Adams, *How to Fail at Almost Everything and Still Win Big: Kind of the Story of My Life,* Penguin Books, New York, 203.

5. "The Upside of Anger," IMDB, accessed 21 December 2015.

6. Ibid.

7. Matthew Wilkening, "29 Years Ago: Def Leppard Drummer Rick Allen Loses Arm in Car Crash," *Ultimate Classic Rock*, December 31, 2013.

8. "Taking Risks" September 10, 2013 blog post, http://project-resiliency .org/blog/taking-risks/.

9. "YD Interview: Arthur Boorman, Disabled Vet Who Lost 140 Pounds and Gained His Life Back Through Yoga," published on YogaDork blog January 10, 29013.

10. Never, Ever Give Up. Arthur's Inspirational Transformation!, YouTube video posted April 30, 2012.

11. "YD Interview: Arthur Boorman, Disabled Vet Who Lost 140 Pounds and Gained His Life Back Through Yoga," published on YogaDork blog January 10, 29013.

12. Lou Dzierzak, "Factoring Fear: What Scares Us and Why," *Scientific American*, October 27, 2008.

13. America's Top Fears 2015, October 13, 2015 press release by the Wilkinson College of Arts, Humanities, and Social Sciences.

14. James Ball, "September 11's Indirect Toll: Road Deaths Linked to Fearful Flyers," *The Guardian*, September 5, 2011.

15. Ibid.

16. Laurence Gonzales, *Deep Survival: Who Lives, Who Dies, and Why*, New York, W.W. Norton & Co. For more on Laurence Gonzales visit www.deepsurvival.com/.

17. "1985 Mexico City earthquake," Wikipedia, accessed December 17, 2015.

18. For more on Bucio's remarkable story visit the website of his medical practice, www.franciscobucio.com/html/biography.html; and www.cpmc.org/advanced/microsurg/procedures/cases.html.

19. Sue Shellenbarger, "When Stress Is Good for You," *The Wall Street Journal*, January 24, 2012.

20. Ibid.

21. Holly C. Corbett, "7 Weird Health Perks of Being Stressed," *Prevention*, April 9, 2012.

22. Kelly McGonigal, "Use Stress to Your Advantage," *The Wall Street Journal*, May 15, 2015.

23. Alison Wood Brooks, "Get Excited: Reappraising Pre-Performance Anxiety as Excitement," *Journal of Experimental Psychology*, Vol. 143, 2014, pp. 1144–1158.

24. Geir Jordet et al., "The BASES Expert Statement on the Psychological Preparation for Football Penalty Shots," *The British Association of Sport and Exercise Sciences*, Winter 2013.

25. "American Psychological Association Survey Shows Money Stress Weighing on Americans' Health Nationwide," American Psychological Association press release, February 4, 2015.

26. Rebecca Knight, "How to Overcome Burnout and Stay Motivated," *Harvard Business Review*, April 2, 2015.

27. Craig Dowden, "A Key to Success-With Interest," *Psychology Today*, June 1, 2014.

Conclusion

On the night of April 29, 1849 *The Hannah,* a brig transporting immigrants fleeing the famine in Ireland sank in the Gulf of Lawrence.[1] Encountering heavy winds the brig struck an ice berg that punched a hole in the hull. Captain Curry Shaw, along with his first and second officers, fled in the only lifeboat leaving the passengers to fend for themselves. To escape the sinking *Hannah* the remaining crewmen helped the passengers onto an ice floe next to the bow.[2] The passengers viewed the very object that caused their tragic event also as a potential life-saving strategy. They climbed onto the ice floe and waited for help to arrive. *The Nicaragua* under the command of Captain William Marshall appeared the next day and rescued the 127 survivors. *The Hannah*'s passengers and crew, like so many others in this book, demonstrated a combination three of the seven characteristics of successful people outlined in this publication. There was no one secret to their survival. They had a bias toward action, engaged with each other, and created options for themselves by viewing the ice floe as a life-saving solution.

Sixty-three years later, on April 14, 1912 the *RMS Titanic* collided with an iceberg in the north Atlantic and sunk in less than three hours leaving just 705 survivors from its 2,200 passengers and crew. While the *Titanic's* passengers and crew used 16 lifeboats and waited for the *Carpathia* to rescue them they ultimately failed to utilize the iceberg as a mean of survival like those from *The Hannah* decades earlier. As Tony McCaffrey and Jim Pearson wrote in the December 2015 issue of *Harvard Business Review* "imagine how many more might have lived if crew members had thought of the iceberg as not just the cause of the disaster but a life-saving solution."[3]

Frederick Buechner, the American writer and theologian wrote "To live is to experience all sorts of things. It would be a shame to experience them—these rich experiences of sadness and happiness and success and failure—and then have it just all vanish, like a dream when you wake up.

Pay attention to your life."[4] One way to "pay attention to your life" is to "repot yourself." The late American writer John Gardner pushed people to think about "repotting" themselves every 10 to 15 years, throwing themselves into challenges that extract hidden strengths. By repotting, people can recreate the sense of excitement and imagination experienced earlier in life. It also has the wonderful side benefit of slowing down time. Repotting makes experiences more vivid as each adventure is filled with firsts: the first few weeks on a new job, the first conversations with new neighbors in a new location and so on. The newness of it all has the potential to heighten senses and deepen memories. Sometimes people stumble upon an opportunity to repot themselves like Bennet Ifeakandu Omalu.

Bennet Ifeakandu Omalu is a Nigerian American forensic pathologist, who examined the brains of several deceased NFL players and was the first to publish findings of chronic traumatic encephalopathy (CTE), a progressive degenerative disease found in people with a history of repetitive brain trauma.[5] Omalu is the central character portrayed by Will Smith in the 2015 film *Concussion*. Omalu needed to repot himself when he conducted an autopsy of former Pittsburgh Steelers center Mike Webster in 2002 and found himself in completely new territory spending several years trying to convince the scientific community and the National Football League of the significance of his findings.[6] Sometimes people stumble upon an opportunity to repot themselves like Omalu. He was working as the Allegheny County Coroner's Office neuropathologist at the time he autopsied Webster and never intended to be at the center of one of the most important sports related issues of the 21st century. Others, however, need to sustain the self-awareness to ask the question: 'is it time to repot myself?'

Is it time to repot yourself? This is perhaps one of the most important questions you can ask yourself. And it is one you should revisit at least once a year. As Ted Turner's father said to him, "Son, you be sure to set your goals so high that you can't possibly accomplish them in one lifetime. That way you'll always have something ahead of you. I made the mistake of setting my goals too low and now I'm having a hard time coming up with new ones."[7] Turner's father would eventually commit suicide and left his young son to move forward without him.[8]

As you finish reading this book, challenge yourself to have as many dreams as you need two lifetimes to achieve them. This will be challenging to do as the pressure from external events like the global economic crisis, geopolitical instability, and severe weather events, just to name a few, will continue to present individuals and organizations with new issues to address, questions to answer, and problems to solve.

As you travel up and down those seven steps remember the characteristics of successful people:

1. *Have a bias toward action*: Successful people have a bias toward action. They pursue what researchers have labeled deliberate practice, they demonstrate some level of maverickism, and they exhibit courageous behavior.
2. *Engage with others*: Successful people engage with others. They engage with a wide spectrum of people to collaborate, they leverage technology to connect with crowds around the globe, and they work and socialize in open networks.
3. *Commit to life-long learning*: Successful people are life-long learners. They possess what researchers have labeled a growth mindset, they understand the focusing illusion, and they develop their emotional intelligence.
4. *Increase your self-awareness*: Successful people increase their self-awareness. They practice a growth mindset, they understand the focusing illusion, and they develop their emotional intelligence.
5. *Remain open to the possibilities*: Successful people remain open to the possibilities. They work hard at determining their self, they understand how to market their value, and they practice meditation.
6. *Create options*: Successful people create options. They assess what is best versus what is right, they know how to turn a disadvantage into an advantage, and they engage in subtle maneuvers.
7. *Maintain a high level of energy*: Successful people maintain a high level of energy. They manage their fear, they practice deep survival tactics, and they perform under pressure.

I wish you well along your journey.

Questions and Resources

- Do you have a bias toward action?
- How often do you expand your ability to collaborate with others?
- What have you done to demonstrate a commitment to lifelong learning?
- How have you increased your level of self-awareness?
- When were you open to new possibilities?
- What have you done to create options?
- What do you do to maintain a high level of energy?

The Success Inventory: Complete the following inventory by asking yourself how often you demonstrated each characteristic during the last _____ (fill in the blank with a time period, e.g., three months). Write down today's date and then periodically complete this inventory and then compare your most recent results with your previous answers.

Example 1: during the last two weeks I very often collaborated with others as my team had a major project to complete at work.

Example 2: during the last two weeks I rarely practiced a growth mindset and told myself I would never be able to learn how to practice yoga since I am too old to do so.

Characteristic	Never	Rarely	Sometimes	Very Often	Always
Engaged in deliberate practice					
Demonstrated maverick traits					
Exhibited courage					
Collaborated					
Leveraged crowds					
Worked in an open network					
Practiced the growth mindset					
Understood the focusing illusion					

Characteristic	Never	Rarely	Sometimes	Very Often	Always
Developed emotional intelligence					
Determined your self					
Marketed your value					
Meditated					
Thought differently					
Experienced disequilibrium					
Remained open to serendipity					
Decided right over best					
Turned a disadvantage into an advantage					
Engaged in subtle maneuvers					
Managed fear					
Learned deep survival tactics					
Performed under pressure					

Many of life's failures are people who did not realize how close they were to success when they gave up.

—Thomas Edison

Endnotes

1. John Kernaghan, "The Hannah: An Irish Odyssey," *Irish America,* April/May 2011.
2. Ibid.
3. Tony McCaffrey and Jim Pearson, "Find Innovation Where You Least Expect It," *Harvard Business Review,* December 2015.
4. Art Carey, "Vanguard founder John Bogle's enduring wisdom," *Philadelphia Inquirer*, September 16, 2013.
5. "Bennet Omalu, *Wikipedia* accessed December 28, 2015.
6. Ibid.
7. Ted Turner and Bill Burke, *Call Me Ted*, Turner Works, LLC, 2008.
8. Jonann Brady and Lee Ferran, "Turner: Tough Father 'Made Me a Better Man,'" *ABC news*, November 11, 2008.

Index

OTHER TITLES IN THE HUMAN RESOURCE MANAGEMENT AND ORGANIZATIONAL BEHAVIOR COLLECTION

- *Fostering Creativity in Self and the Organization: Your Professional Edge* by Eric W. Stein
- *Designing Creative High Power Teams and Organization: Beyond Leadership* by Eric W. Stein
- *Creating a Pathway to Your Dream Career: Designing and Controlling a Career Around Your Life Goals* by Tom Kucharvy
- *Leader Evolution: From Technical Expertise to Strategic Leadership* by Alan Patterson
- *Followership: What It Takes to Lead* by James H. Schindler
- *The Search For Best Practices: Doing the Right Thing the Right Way* by Rob Reider
- *Marketing Your Value: 9 Steps to Navigate Your Career* by Michael Edmondson
- *Competencies at Work: Providing a Common Language for Talent Management* by Enrique Washington and Bruce Griffiths
- *Manage Your Career: 10 Keys to Survival and Success When Interviewing and on the Job, Second Edition* by Vijay Sathe
- *You're A Genius: Using Reflective Practice to Master the Craft of Leadership* by Steven S. Taylor
- *Major in Happiness: Debunking the College Major Fallacies* by Michael Edmondson
- *The Resilience Advantage: Stop Managing Stress and Find Your Resilience* by Richard S. Citrin and Alan Weiss

Announcing the Business Expert Press Digital Library

Concise e-books business students need for classroom and research

This book can also be purchased in an e-book collection by your library as

- a one-time purchase,
- that is owned forever,
- allows for simultaneous readers,
- has no restrictions on printing, and
- can be downloaded as PDFs from within the library community.

Our digital library collections are a great solution to beat the rising cost of textbooks. E-books can be loaded into their course management systems or onto student's e-book readers.

The **Business Expert Press** digital libraries are very affordable, with no obligation to buy in future years. For more information, please visit **www.businessexpertpress.com/librarians.** To set up a trial in the United States, please contact **sales@businessexpertpress.com.**

www.ingramcontent.com/pod-product-compliance
Lightning Source LLC
Chambersburg PA
CBHW060544210326
41519CB00014B/3339